Edited 10/2013
First print 10/2013

BOOKSTORE DISTRIBUTION Contact:
Urbansoup2020@gmail.com

Place orders via our e-mail.

ISBN-13: 978-1497593879
ISBN-10: 1497593875

Printed in the United States of America

Acknowledgments

A Taste Of Urban For The People' s Soul

B-More Loyals

A Taste Of Urban Soup
For The People's Soul
Real life stories too open and shed light into the hearts and
re- kindle all spirits.

Christopher White, Chandra White, Pamela White

Dedication

This book is dedicated to the Lord Jesus Christ. For making life possible for the many people who gave a real life account of the things they have experienced in their lives and how God was always present. This book is also dedicated to each and every person who supports this project to help us to donate 10% of every book sold all over the world to help sponsor (Aids Awareness, Cancer Awareness, Battered Women, Rape Victims, Missing Children, and each and every one in the world that pray and seek God. This project is how people will get to see that Jesus Christ is alive and still into answering prayers.

Bible Verse
The book of Job

Chapter 1 selected verses . . .1 In the land of Uz there lived a man whose name was Job. This man was blameless and upright; he feared God and shunned evil. Verse 6. One day the angels came to present themselves before the Lord, and Satan also came with them.

The Lord said to Satan, "Where have you come from?"

Satan answered the Lord, "From roaming through the earth and going back and forth in it."

Then the Lord said to Satan, "Have you considered my servant Job? There is no one on earth like him; he is blameless and upright, a man who fears God and shuns evil. 9. "Does Job fear God for nothing?"

Satan replied. 10. Have you not put a hedge around him and his household and everything he has? You have blessed the work of his hands, so that his flocks and herds are spread throughout the land. 11. But stretch out your hand, and strike everything he has, and he will surely curse you to your face."

12. The Lord said to Satan, "Very well, then, everything he has is in your hands, but on the man himself do not lay a finger."

Then Satan went out from the presence of the Lord. Just wanted to share that Satan don't have no power but what the Lord allow him to have over us.

Introduction

To God be the glory. I'm truly honored and blessed to be able to be a part of this Urban Soup movement. To be able to create this book, and allow people all over the world to get "A Taste of Urban Soup for The People' s Soul. " This has been a great walk being able to sit down and interview real people and see what they have been through. It has been all love. This project and every project the author do is always divinely inspired. When the dream was conceived, I knew that it was the power of the Holy Spirit giving direction. I know it's God because I was never supposed to be born, so I'm a miracle. Reading the bible has showed me about the talents and gifts that everyone has, and the bible teaches us all how to tap into the powers we all have. I pray that everyone will put their trust in God and depend on the Lord for everything.

Testimony Of My Life

*****Based On A True Story*****

Preface

"Girl, get your butt in here right now!"

Pam said, "No mommy!" Pam got a beating for running out in the middle of the street earlier that day.

Momma was determined to teach Pam about not listening to her about her getting hit by a car.

Pam was just a li'l girl, 5 years old, beautiful lil girl, very smart, but she wasn't thinking at that moment.

After Momma had beaten her lil butt, she ran outside and climbed into Momma's car as she so often did. Pam always found peace sitting inside of the car. She would be praying and talking with God a lot, but since the beating she just didn't feel like praying at the time. She just sat inside of the car with her mind racing 100 miles an hour. Pam decided that she wanted to strike a bunch of matches this night. Pam struck match after match, just letting them burn all the way down to the very tip. Pam lit another match and this time as she watched the fire burn down, Momma walked to the door, and Pam took her eyes off of the match. It fell out of her hand and instantly the entire inside of the car caught flames. Pam was trapped inside, she was scared to death, she was screaming for God to save her. Momma ran to the car trying to get Pam out of the burning car, she was screaming for her life, she was crying something out of this world. Pam was burning up in that car. Momma was crying and screaming for help. She couldn't get the car door to open up, or maybe Pam had locked the doors when she got into the car. A nearby neighbor heard all of the screaming and commotion. She looked out of the window to see the car on fire and she called for help.

911 Operator, "How may I help you?" "There's a car on fire with a li'l girl trapped inside." She gave the street and address.

The operator said, "That help was on the way."

The fire department got there in the nick of time to save Pam's life.

Momma was no more good, her one and only li'l girl was burned beyond recognition. She was skinless.

Pam was unconscious, not moving, she wasn't dead, but she wasn't moving at all. Her body had no skin at all, her hair was all gone, no eye brows, and there was nothing but bleeding flesh. She arrived at the hospital where doctors went right to work on her as soon as she came into the building.

One doctor broke down crying at how badly Pam had gotten burned up. The scene was unbearable. Momma had already passed out. Doctors had to keep her under observation and she had lost all since of direction. The best part about this was that God was still with Pam and He still was present through it all. God is always there, even when we can't see or feel Him. He's still amazing. Pam stayed in the hospital for months, praying all day and night long, thanking God for saving her life and never leaving her. Pam loved the Lord to death and she never ever blamed God or got mad at Him. The doctors were human, and people let us down all the time, but trust in God . . . He is faithful, amazing, good, and true, and there is no one like Him, Sweet, Loyal, and He never ever gives up on us. The head doctor told Pam and Momma that she was burned so bad that she would never ever in life be able to have any children. It crushed Pam to hear those words coming from the doctor. Pam cried and cried, but Pam knew that God had the final say so in all things. She trusted in God's word.

Pam got older and she started to get back to herself. Taking good care of her wounds, she pressed on. After all that Pam had endured, she became a great woman and she met a man one day, who God sent to her. They married, and despite the odds against her, or what man said she couldn't or wouldn't be able to do, she was blessed beyond her wildest dreams. Pam was blessed to have a son and she called him (Christopher White, Jr.). She knew that this child was never ever supposed to be born into this world according to man and the doctor who told her this when she was but a li'l girl. She knew that this child was never to be sitting at the computer emailing the world and his friends on Facebook this testimony, but she knew that God was in full control, not man. Not only did God bless Pam with li'l Chris, He gave her two more girls, (Alicia & Christine White). This is my word for today. As people we are to never trust in what man tells us about ourselves. We have to stay in prayer and seeking the answers that we so desire from above...

Put your trust in Jesus Christ. Man will let us down every time, but God will perform that which He have started in us. God is my everything trusts in Him and Him alone. God's word says so in the Bible in Psalm 37:3-5. Verse 3 says, "Trust in the Lord, and do good; dwell in the land, and feed on His faithfulness. "Verse 4 stated, "Delight yourself also in the Lord, and He shall give you the desires of your heart." Verse 5 says, "Commit your way to the Lord, trust also in Him, and He shall bring it to pass." I pray that this testimony may help just one person and help you to see that God doesn't make mistakes, He has a plan for us all, even me. When the doctor said I was not supposed to be born, but you sitting right there at your computer reading my emails and my Facebook postings right now. I have written books about the life that a man told my mother she wouldn't have. So you tell me who is right and wrong. I'm already spoken for and will never again be available but my work for the Lord is never ending. I'm here for you in more ways then you will ever be able to grasp. If you need help to repair your marriage, relationship, friendship, reading your word, or whatever it is that you need help with, you have my attention and devotion to helping God's people, my people. Right now I'm in the belly of the beast, but I'm doing better in the beast then a lot of others are. They claim to have it all together, but if you don't have Jesus Christ then you don't anything together. Jesus Christ is the only way to God. Well, I hope and pray that this has helped someone. As a matter of fact, this story broke me done like a "57" Chevy truck last night as I read this to one of my friends that's in here with me. It messed him up to. I pray that the Lord will keep my family and loved one's safe and the rest of the world as well. I ask all this in the mighty name of Jesus Christ. .... Amen. My first book will be out soon, but you can read the first few chapters on my Facebook page right now. Read it, hit me back with your feedback, and let me know what you think of my old life because God had done away with the old and I'm a new man in Christ. I need you; just as well as you think that you need me. I'm that friend that the Lord wants to use to you know that He is real. Remember God saw all of this afar off, man didn't see it. I'm here satan and you don't have any power over my life anymore. I'm working for God now and forevermore. So my friends leave me your email information and I'll be happy to help you with whatever it is that's bothering you. With prayer and fasting I know that I can go to God and have your answers.... In the name of Jesus Christ with my lips I say Amen.

Chapter Two
***** Down but Not Out *****

Dear Readers,

My name is Christopher White and a lot of people that are reading this in the Fed's, ya'll know me as Rich Boy. At this present time, I'm down, meaning that, yes, I'm locked up physically; meaning my body, but, people, my mind is as sharp as a razor fresh out of a box cutter. I'm serving a 30-year sentence, been in this setback since 1998. So, yea, I'm down, but not out.

Being in here, people, I've had a chance to find and get to know that real me, without all of the drug money, cars, and girls. Yes, I can admit it now, people. I was lost and chasing after a dream that never ever came true. So, yes, I'm down, but not out.

Being down has afforded me a great second chance at life, and what I mean by that is this right here. People, prison has saved me. I know, your reading this and saying to yourself, Chris is tripping, right? Well I'm not, just keeping it real. People, prison has never ever been about four cement walls and a steel door. Prison is a place of consecration. It's a place where God gives us a timeout. Because I was headed to hell, He loved me so much that He took me and hid me so that I could get my mind right.

Prison, for me, has been a place of redemption from the wickedness of my own soul. The streets of B-More would have killed me, if God hadn't saved me: Life recreates physically that which you live for mentally. I mistrusted my own self which caused me to place myself in the predicament of mistrusting others and my surroundings. Prison is about trusting in me: Trust in my own self, Trust in my own ideas, Dreams, and Abilities: Trusting in God and living like Jesus Christ my Lord. Prison is really about, if not you, then who? If not now, then when, people? Who can change our lives if God can't? When do we make a great decision to accept the Lord Jesus to change us and make us right? If not today and if not right here, right now, when? People, we can't change yesterday, but we can soon soar to new highs with God in full control of our lives. We can never ever forget the pains of yesterday either.

We can trust in Jesus Christ and allow God to have His way with us and be down and not out, but be down and still on top!! I'm down, people, but not out. Actually, I pray this article can save just one life, or many. I'm down but, I'm down with Jesus Christ. God has blessed me with another chance at life.

I've finished school, something that I would have never done on the streets. It's people who are not down physically, but who are down mentally and spiritually that I wish to reach. I'm down, but free as a bird flying to wherever it wants to fly to. I'm down, right, but I'm now writing on my 5th book. My first book is called, "B-More Loyal/30 Years Before Dishonor." It's coming out really soon. I'm down, but I've accomplished more than a lot of people that look down on the ones that are in prison. I've done more than a lot of people will do and they say that they are free. I'm down, but I'm on my way to make it to the bestselling author's list, selling books worldwide; The reason is because God is my Rock and I'm now operating in the spirit.

Being down has afforded me the chance to search within myself and tap into hidden talents that I never knew existed. God has put talents inside of all of us. Being down is what we make it to be. I'm working even though I'm down.

I have fulfilled one of my many dreams, and I see people who are free and still can't get ahead. They are free physically, but they are out. I have a Facebook page setup for you to go onto and check out the first 4 chapters of my books. Go to: bmoreloyal360@gmail.com. You can follow me on that link. The Book "B-More Loyal" is a great book and you'll keep turning page after page. It's a must read, my friends. Here' s a li'l short story about being down, but not out.

"Tim - Tim, report to the visiting room now. This is your last call."

Oh shoot man that's me that they are calling. I have to go. Tim got up and ran to the unit so that he could take a quick shower and get himself ready. The officer working the unit opened the door for Tim and said "Inmate Smith, where have you been for the past 30 minutes?"

"Oh my fault, I was in the music room and I wasn't expecting anyone to come to see me today . . . C.O., but I see that someone came. I just need 10 minutes to get ready; can you tell the visiting room officer that I'm on my way, please, sir?"

"I'll do it for you this one time and you better make this your last time, because I will not do it again."

"Thank you, sir," and Tim ran up the stairs to shower and get dressed for this visit that he was not prepared for.

"Okay C.O. I'm ready to go! "

The C.O. asked Tim, "Do you have your I.D. card?" "Yes, I have it sir."

"Compound, I have an inmate for visit coming from B-4 unit, can I send him?"

"10-4, copy."

"The officer opened the door and Tim rolled out to go to the visiting room. Once Tim got to the visiting room he knocked on the door. The visiting room officer opened the door and let Tim in. Once he was inside the strip room, there was two other officers inside of the room standing there with riot gear on, with clubs in their hands. Tim was scared to death, but he stood there to see what was going on.

Tim asked the officer, "Sir, may I enter the visiting room, please, to see my people?"

The officer looked at Tim in a crazy way. Then one of the other officers that was wearing the riot gear spoke up.

"I received a cop-out telling me that you have been sleeping with my wife. "

Tim stood there for a moment and as he was trying to grasp and understand how he was being set up by someone, the officer walked over to Tim and smacked him with a club. Blood spurted everywhere. Tim was screaming now as the other officer came up and started hitting him, kicking him, beating him with no mercy. The beating was so bad that Tim was going in and out of consciousness.

"What the heck is going on here, " Tim said as the dream came to an end. When he awoke, he was soaking wet from sweating. His cell was so dark. He had put his coat in the window to block out the extra light from shining in through his cell window. Tim just laid there, heart beating faster than ever before, and all out of control. He thought about the C.O. 's wife who worked over in the education department that he' s been laying wood in to.

Tim said, "To himself, man, I have to leave this woman alone for real. "

Quick li'l short story about being down, but not out, but on top. Follow me on my Facebook page ....

Email: bmoreloyal360@gmail.com

"B-More Loyal/30 Years Before Dishonor"

**** Letter From The Author****

Christopher White 33352-037
P.O. Box 7000
Texarkana, TX 75505

Greetings,

My name is Christopher White, I' am 37 years old, and I' am from Baltimore, Maryland. There I grew up in a single parent home, where my mother was battling with substance abuse. That lead me to rely on the streets for guidance, not having any positive role model in my life caused the start of my adult life to lead me to prison. I thank God for loving me and allowing me this time to get my life right. God has used this setback as a major come back; therefore, He could get the glory through my Urban/Christian novels that I have penned. God has blessed me with a gift to write great books to help our world to see that people can change. These books show my negative actions that have a positive result. Many times we go through life trying to do things on our own. As a ex-drug dealer, I know it was the Holy Spirit that changed me. My books present a message of how God was working in my life while I was still in my mess.

My goal is to bring about a spiritual awareness to build a great spiritual kingdom for those who have experienced the same journey as I.

Yours In Christ ...

Chapter 1
***** Respect My Hustle*****

"Mail call, mail call, "Romie heard the C.O. saying mail call, but he thought that he was dreaming. He has been waiting on this to come a few weeks now. Shorty got up and ran downstairs to see if he was called for anything at mail call or not.

"Yo, Black did you hear the C.O. call my name or Eric's name yet?"

Black said, "Naw Yo, I have not heard anything yet, I had just now walked up here. Alright then Yo, we need this thing to get here today. Yo they said that they sent it a few weeks ago now it should have been here by now. "

Romie turned around and he started calling for Eric. "Yo, Eric, Yo, Eric, " the C.O. had called Eric' s name like four times for mail now, and Romie's eyes were glistening now just seeing all of the different magazines. Then the C.O. called Romie's name four times right behind Eric's name. That was the cue that everything went through for him and the rest of all the B-More dudes that were rolling with the B-More car on the compound. Romie kept on calling for Eric so that he could bring his butt on down stairs so that he could get this mail that contained the dope. The B-More boyz had F.C.I. Beckley on smash. This pack of goons had all of the stamps on the compound, and a ticket that was moving well. Just like the streets these niggas were known all over the jails and across the Fed's and worldwide for putting in that work. In the streets they were known for having guns and it changes in the prison system. They were known for having knives and stabbing anyone in a heartbeat who disrespected them. Black was standing there just knowing by instinct and body language that

Romie was on the move again. It was again time for him to go and get those joints back out of the stash and have them sharp and ready to be worked if need be. Black was always on point like Stacy Adams. He was always on the frontline whenever it came to his homies from B-More. They all knew that Romie was trying to lock the compound down so that the B-More car would have everything that they needed. Romie was mad as ever because Eric was slipping, knowing good and dag on well that he was supposed to have his butt down stairs at the mail call every day. Romie sent Big Head to Eric's cell to see why the heck he had not made it down stairs to mail call and picked up the magazines that contained the dope. Sneaky ran upstairs along with Big Head and when they came to Eric's cell, he had the towel up covering the cell window. Big Head scanned the unit to find that Eric's cellie was down stairs already playing chess with someone at the table, but Big Head could hear all kinds of noise coming through the cell door like something or someone was in trouble inside of Eric's cell. Sneaky and Big Head looked at each other and decided since Eric was their homie, they could just barge into Eric's cell since his cellie was down stairs. They wanted to see if their homie was okay. They wanted to see why he had not showed up for mail call. Big Head turned the knob to the cell and they both stepped into the cell to find Eric on his knees sucking big Jino off. Big Head was stuck in his tracks and Sneaky just couldn't believe what the heck he had just seen. Eric was so embarrassed that he was caught. Big Jino was embarrassed as well. Big Jino had heard the rumors of him having sex with men in prison, but now he knew from experience, it was true. Eric couldn't believe that his li'l fling and secret was all the way out of the bag now. He had denied it every time that it ever came up to him. Eric was confronted on numerous occasions by the B- More car about them having gumps rolling with them, but Eric always puffed up his chest and said that someone was just hating on him, or jealous. He stuck to his lie that he was all

17

man and that he would out that knife in whoever was lying on him about messing with boyz. As Big Head and Sneaky walked towards where Romie was waiting for Eric so that he could get the mags with the dope in it, Big Head had tears in his eyes because he knew that the entire B-More car really liked Eric. He would buck about going up top, despite the B-More car having messing with boyz or hot niggas running around on the compound with them like stuff sweet. Big Head just knew that since he was the one that witnessed this act, he would have to be the one that put the work in on Eric, if he didn't' check in on his own. Romie was fuming now, "Yo, where the heck that nigga Eric at? Sneaky why ya'll looking all crazy like ya'll have lost your best friend or something?" Sneaky said, "Yo go on and tell him Big Head." Romie said, "tell me what?" By this time all of the B-More dudes were coming up into Romie's unit. Everyone knew that it was time to get their shine on again. Eric came walking down stairs looking all crazy. The C.O. was now standing outside of the unit, because the compound was now open for a five-minute rec. move, and that's how at least 20 more B-More dudes had arrived inside of Romie's unit. As Eric walked up to join the Baltimore car, Romie repeated himself again, "Tell me what, Sneaky." "Naw, there he go, there go Eric right there. "Romie walked up on Eric and swung on him, connecting on the side of his head. Eric grabbed Romie, but everyone converged on them to break it up. Sneaky, said, "Yo, Eric, you need to go ahead and go get them mag's for Romie and then you have to go up top. " Eric looked at Sneaky saying, "And what, you going to make me go up nigga?" Then Big Head got involved and he said, "Naw, nigga, I'm going to stab you up and send you in or you can walk to the Lt's office and make this easy on yourself; make it easier and clean or make it harder and bloody. It's your call, my nigga. "The entire B-More car was caught off guard with all that had just taken place. Romie cut in and said, "Yo, you need to get that mail. "Eric walked up to the C.O. 's office to get the magazines that contained the dope. While he was gone Big Head told Romie that after Eric brought him the mags he would have to go in, but Romie wasn't understanding where all of this extra action was coming from. Romie knew that it was way more to this story then met the eyes, so he asked Big Head what the heck was up. Big Head said, "I'll let you ask Eric when he comes back down from getting the mail." Romie just stood there with this puzzled look on his face wondering what had happened from the time of mail call and Big Head's going to Eric's cell. Big Head turned to Low-Low and asked him, "Yo, Low, you strapped."

He said, "You know it."

"Yo, give me your knife. I'm going to have to put some work in today." Romie was heated now, but Eric came walking up with the mags in his hands. Romie said, "Yo, Eric, what' s up?" Eric said, "These niggas tripping, walking all up into my cell without knocking, violating my space." Big Head asked him, "So Eric what's up we going to do this the easy way or the hard way, it's your call my nigga?" Romie stepped to Big Head who had just reached under his shirt and pulled out the knife that he got from Low-Low. This joint wasn't just a average size knife, he had a sword in his hand. Big Head was now wrapping the security string around his hand to put Eric out of his misery. Sneaky just hopped down off of the railing and said, "Look Eric, you a gump, we caught you just now on your knees giving that faggot nigga Jino head." Everyone looked at Eric now, he didn't say anything at all to try and help or to defend himself. The C.O. came out of his office to unlock the unit door since it was now chow time for the unit. The compound officer had just called the unit for chow and everyone was starting to leave the unit so the C.O. stepped outside. Romie looked at Eric and said, "Oh yea, Yo, you on butt now. I been hearing that but I would've never in a million years believed that crap about you, Yo, "Romie said, "Yo, give me my mags and go ahead over to lock up, Yo." Eric gave Romie the mags and stood his ground. "Ya'll going to have to put me in the hole then, because I'm not doing no checking in, my nigga." Big head moved quickly and grabbed Eric and started stabbing him up. Eric tried to swing back, but the goons were all on him like bees on honey. Eric was screaming because Big Head was driving that sword into his head, back, arms, and legs. Blood was everywhere. Eric's clothes had changed from white and gray, to a dark, dark red, deep color red. Eric was hollering for help and spitting up a lot of blood. Big Head had hit Eric around 30 times with that big ole sword. Big Head gave the knife back to Low-Low and he wiped it off and rolled out to go and put it back in his stash spot. As the B-More goons were all leaving, Romie ran up to his cell and put the dope up after he had broken down each magazine and torn the pages apart. He had it all stashed.

Romie said, "Wow, Yo sent us 15 grams this time. Romie was happy about this lick right here. Just as he was coming back down stairs, the C.O. was coming back into the unit and he saw all of the blood with Eric lying in a pool of blood. The C.O. hit the deuces and the other officers from across the compound came running to assist the officers in the Eric's unit. He also announced through the walkie-talkie that it was a man down and he needs serious medical attention. Romie was upstairs trying to put the dope in the proper stash that he had inside of his cell and he got caught in the lock down that was coming next. He knew they were in for a lock down for at least a few hours. Romie had it in mind that while they were locked down for a few hours, he was going to use his combination lock and crush up the rocks in the dope, then he'd empty out a few rice bags and cut them up into 50 dollar pieces. When they come off of lock down, shop was going to be wide open. Romie already knew that since it was a black on black thing they would open the compound right back up. The only way they would stay on lock down for weeks at a time was if it was another race against another race. That was a major lock down. He went to get everything ready so he could make this money the entire compound was waiting on the Baltimore dudes to make this move. The Crip's, Indians, Blood's, Dirty White Boyz, and all of the other people on the compound were waiting to cop this raw dope to come up or to get high. Whoever wanted to get money had to come through Romie and the B- More car to get it. Romie would be selling grams for 1,000 dollars apiece. Depending on how many pieces a person brought at one time, the would sometimes drop the price. Romie was the master mind behind getting his work into any prison.

Chapter 2
***** Respect My Hustle *****

Meanwhile on lock down, D.C. Rob was lying in his bunk trying to scam up a way to get 10 books of stamps so that he could get high. He knew each book of stamps was going for $5.00 a book, and his broke cellie wanted to get high with him. Big O from D.C. started washing stamps. He took all of his mail out of his locker and started peeling the old stamps off of the letters that he had accumulated over the months. Big O told Rob to help him with peeling all of the stamps off the letters. Somehow Big O had come across some alcohol and he used that to erase all the post office black lines that showed the stamps as being used.

Chapter 3
***** Respect My Hustle *****

Big head was nervous and praying hard that he hadn't killed Eric, if ever Big Head didn't trust or believe in God, he sure did now. Big Head already knew that the 15 years that he had now would only turn into a life sentence. The new law now was that if any inmate who was already serving time caught murder charge while incarcerated he would get a life sentence that would override what he was already serving. Big Head was not happy at all about the outcome of the scene right now. Big Head couldn't stop pacing the cell floor. His cellie knew that something was wrong but he just laid his butt down. Big Head had blood all on his clothes and boots. He was so scared that he forgot to inspect himself, in case upper body searches were called for in every unit on the compound. Big Head's cellie finally got up the nerve to say something to him. "Dag cellie, you look like you been in a war."

Big Head stopped pacing and walked over to the top bunk. "What did you say to me punk?"

Drake said, "Look at your clothes cellie, you got blood all over you."

Big Head stepped back and looked himself over and went straight into panic mode, "Oh man, help me out cellie." Drake jumped off of the bunk and helped Big Head to clean his-self up.

Chapter 4
***** Respect My Hustle *****

Help had arrived at the unit for Eric who was now lying stiff as a bird. He wasn't dead but he wasn't moving either. Medical had to reach the Federal Marshall's office because this was too serious to deal with at the prison medical hospital. The prison Warden had to call for a helicopter to save Eric's life. He was hit up pretty badly. Big Head had worked Eric over, all because he was caught up messing with another man while in prison. There is a code in prison and certain things just have to get dealt with. The Lt. was heated that a stabbing had to happen and be this gruesome and life threatening on his watch. The Lt. called for upper body searches for the entire compound, and inside of the kitchen as well. The chow hall had plenty of people there as well. Romie had his cellie Dre watching out for him at the cell door window. Dre kept an eye on the C.O.'s to see where they were starting. They were getting closer and closer to Romie's cell so he had to put everything away, then they sat and listened to their radio, waiting on the C.O.'s to check their bodies.

Dre said, "Romie what the heck happened out there earlier?"

Romie replied, "I'm really not sure, but Big Head put some work in on the homie Eric. They said something about him messing with boyz and it was on."

Dre said "I had heard a few times, but you know how niggas be saying anything when niggas doing their thing, getting money and they can't get none." The Lt. got to Romie's cell and they popped his cell.

The C.O. shouted, "Shirts off, open you mouths, let me see your hands, raise your arms, turn around." They were clean. Then the Lt. looked at Romie and asked him, "What happened to the guy down stairs, he's from B-More right?"

Romie said, "I don't know, I was in here writing, then I heard lock down.

"Okay, I'll be seeing you," and the Lt. and his men locked the cell back and continued on with the upper body searched.

Chapter 5
Respect My Hustle

The Indians were geeking, and hoping that this lock down was isolated, and normal would resume in a li'l bit. They wanted to get a few bags of that raw dope. They were sick and needed their fix. Everyone knew that they were getting ready to get that good, good from the B-More car, but nobody could understand what this lock down was all about. Everyone was fiening for the dope. The Indians always spent big bucks getting their fix.

Chapter 6
Respect My Hustle

Big O and Rob had almost 10 books of old washed up stamps. Big O knew that the B-More car wasn't to be played with but they were trying to get high and would do any and everything to get their fix. They were even risking getting into an all-out war to get their fix.

Chapter 7
***** Respect My Hustle *****

Eric was now in surgery where the doctors had worked on him for hours. Eric had lost so much blood. One of his kidneys had been hit. The doctors had to operate to try and fix the small knife hole that they found. They weren't trying to lose him due to an internal bleeding that they could stop, so they went to work on him in the operating room. The Fed's had now arrived at the hospital investigating this case of attempted murder. They knew that Eric being from Baltimore, they had their work cut out for them. This was not going to be an easy case. They had to do all of the work. There were other Federal agents who had arrived at the prison to find out the details of what happened to cause this massive stabbing. The Lt. and other C.O.'s did their questioning, but like always nobody saw anything or heard anything.

"Compound to Lt., go ahead. We have done searches in all the housing units and we're on the last unit right now sir, and nobody shows to have been involved. "

"10-4 copy that, call me again when the last unit has been searched.

"10-4, sir," and they ended the walkie-talkie talk. Lt. said, "I can't keep the pound on lock down, we don't have anything."

Chapter 8
Respect My Hustle

Romie whipped out the bags and had Dre to stand at the doorway to block for him while he bagged up the $50's to get this money as soon as the pound got cleared and opened back up. Romie took his lock and kept on rolling it over top of the rocks in the dope to make sure the dope got fine. Romie was a master mind. He bagged up one gram and he came up with 46 bags from one gram of dope. That was big money! Romie was making more money in prison then the dope boyz were making out there in the real streets. Romie cleaned up the mess and told his cellie to make up 3 lists of commissary food so that they could fill up their lockers. He should make up all 3 lists for sum of $290 dollars apiece. Romie was getting $900 dollars in all commissary food. They was cooking every day of the week, Romie never ever went into the kitchen to eat.

Chapter 9
Respect My Hustle

      Drake helped Big Head out a lot because if he wasn't in the cell with him to see all of the blood all over his clothes and boots, he would be caught up and would be in the hole right now. He changed his uniform and put on some tennis shoes. He wiped his black institution boots off well. You could see the blood all over those boots before Drake had told him about it. All of the other B-More dudes were mad at the fact that Big Head had stabbed Eric. They didn't know that Big Head had caught Eric in the act of sucking a nigga's Johnson Swanson.

Chapter 10
Respect My Hustle

The kitchen still had a lot of inmates inside that were getting restless looking out of the windows wondering what in the world had happened. Compound had hit the Lt. back, told him things were clear and that nobody seemed to have had anything to do with it. No signs of anyone fighting or blood anywhere. The Lt. gave the orders to resume normal activity on the compound. Compound relayed this to all unit officers and they resumed normal operations. The unit officers started to go and re-unlock their unit's.

Chapter 11
Respect My Hustle

Meanwhile, Eric was still in the I.C.U... He had made it through. Eric had tubes all over his body and down his throat, but was still unconscious.

Chapter 12
Respect My Hustle

Big O and Rob knew that this next move was getting ready to cause an all-out war. Baltimore & D.C. war, but they were geeking and needed some dope badly. Big O and Rob came out with 6 books. They were planning on going to cop from Romie's cellie, Dre. He was always amped up about serving and having big books in his possession. As Romie was leaving, he left 20 bags with Dre and he carried 26 bags with him to the rec. yard. As Big O and Rob watched Romie go to the rec. yard, they snuck into Romie's unit to holla at Dre. All of the different cars had come out to rec. to see what was up with Romie and was everything a go or not. The Indian's and White Boyz were trying to go right then and there. They all had mad books of stamps on them at the rec. yard. Black was already on the rec. yard when Romie walked up.

"Yo I brought them joints out here too."

"That's what's up, we are going to need them. I bagged up a few joints." The Indian's walked over to Romie asking him if things were ready. Romie said, "Yea, we all good. Give me a minute and I'll send someone over to you." The Indian's eyes was glistening with pure happiness because he was getting ready to get his blast from the past. The Indian's walked over to the hand ball court.

"We on my nigga," Ron-Ron was the one who did all of the hitting on that compound with the dope bags. He went into the bathroom stall inside the rec. and Romie walked in

33

with him, gave him the packs and told him it was 26 joints inside the pack as he handed the paper towel to Ron-Ron.

"Yo, I'll grab the stamps from everyone and put a number up for the count. The Indian dude's wants three joints already. I just now hollered at them. I'll grab their stamps and send them with you so that ya'll can walk around the track and hit them off."

"Bet that," said Ron-Ron.

Chapter 13
***** Respect My Hustle*****

Meanwhile, back at the unit Dre was called and he came downstairs. He was greeted by Big O and Rob. Rob said, "Yo, where Romie at I heard that he back on with that good." Yo he just went out to the rec. yard, ya'll just now missed him."

"I got 10 books Dre, we are ill as ever, man I swear I don't feel like walking all the way down to rec. Yo, take these 10 books and give me a bag so we can go chill out."

"Okay", said Dre, "Give me the 10 books. I'll do this for you just this one time, but I can't do it ever again." Rob reached into his coat pocket and pulled out the 6 books of washed stamps and the 4 books of plain paper. Dre grabbed the fake books and ran upstairs without even counting the stamps or anything. He was trusting Rob that it was all right, but in prison you can't trust anyone. Dre came right back with the bag of dope and gave it to Rob. He and Big O rolled out laughing saying how they just beat Dre with them fake books. They got to their unit and took their lock and crushed the rest of the rocks that were still in the dope. They wanted to make it as fine as they could get it. They started sniffing the dope and it was pure raw. They both were sitting there high as Fat Charlie, their eyes closing and the dope was like that to. Dre went upstairs and started counting the stamps, but as he counted the stamps he could tell that something wasn't right with these stamps. As he kept on counting he got to all of the white paper and his blood was now boiling to 100 degrees. Dre said a prayer to God because he already knew that he was getting ready to have to put in some work, because these crusty D.C. niggas tried to play him. He walked over to where the knife stash was at to get the joint, but it wasn't there where Romie always kept it. He hid the other bags and got madder and madder. They called the 10-minute move and he shot out of the unit with lightning speed. Romie had sold every last bag that he had brought out to rec. today and there was so many more books on standby out at rec. Romie just made 260 books of stamps in no time. That was a quick 1,300 dollars. Black was laughing at how shock Romie was looking. He was wondering how in the world was he going to make it back to his unit with all of those books of stamps. Then Romie saw his cellie Dre, who was mad as I don't know what. Romie knew that something had happened to his cellie.

Romie said, "Yo, what's up, I know that look. What did she do now?" Romie knew it had something to do with his crazy baby mother who he stayed into it with. "Go ahead spit it out to me, what did she do to you?" Dre said, "She didn't do anything to me where that joint at?" His voice was hard when he asked Romie for the joint. It was the most serious voice Romie had ever heard his cellie talk in. Romie knew that it had really been serious if Dre was asking him for a joint. Dre continued, "Yo I wasn't never ever suppose to serve anyone in the first place, but Big 0 & Rob came looking for you saying that they was ill. I told them that you had went to rec. and they said that they had just missed you. So I tried to look out for them this one time and they played me."

Romie looked at Black who was standing there listening attentively to everything that Dre had just said to Romie. Black liked Dre even though they never had a chance to really sit down and chop it up. He liked the fact that he had heart to go up against those D.C. dudes that tried to play him out. He was a part of the D.M.V... He rocked out for D.C., Maryland, and Virginia. Black asked Dre, "What did they play you with?" Dre said, "I served them a bag of dope and they gave me 6 books of re-used stamps with all paper in the middle of the books Angrily Romie said, "Oh yea, they

36

getting down like that huh. Well on the next move we beefing then. Nothing to talk about. I'm getting ready to set the tone around the pound right now." He continued, "When they call this move it's on, on sight."

Black asked Dre, "Are you sure that you want to handle this like that or what, because you know that if I pass you this joint ain't no turning back Dre."

"Man Black them niggas tried to play me and I'm going to handle my business you feel me."

"So let me ask you then, once again we rocking and rolling Dre." Asked Black?

"Yea, I'm going to set my stage this one time so that word gets out that I'm not to be messed with."

Romie said, "Well we going to them niggas unit then and put this work in and make it back down here to rec. I have to run to the unit to put these books up."

Chapter 14
*****Respect My Hustle*****

Meanwhile, waiting on the move to be called, all the rest of the Baltimore dudes came over to see what was up with Black and Romie. It was like 29 dudes all huddled up together. Black passed Dre the sword. Dre tucked the joint and the other B- More dudes asked what's up? We got beef?

Yea, said Romie, "We got beat by them D.C. clowns and they think it's sweet, they played Dre with some fake books of stamps that they cleaned and a lot of paper. "The entire car was heated by that stunt.

"Yo, we all rocking down there. Who was it anyway?"

"That no good nigga Big O and Rob, and they cellie's to so that's 2 birds with one stone."

Chapter 15
*****Respect My Hustle*****

Eric was in the hospital being questioned by the Fed's. He couldn't do too much talking right now. He just laid there and looked around. Eric laid there wishing that he would have just died. Then all of a sudden he began to cry and it was the hand of God that had touched him. He started to pray and talk to God about what's been going on in his life. He repented and asked God to please forgive him for sinning and everything, even the ones that he had committed in the past as well. Eric thanked the Lord for giving him new life. He knew that the situation was bad, but he also knew that God could channel this bad situation into something great.

Chapter 16
*****Respect My Hustle*****

"Begin 10-minute move."

"Everyone headed for Big o and Rob's unit, accept for Romie who went to his unit to put the books that he had just made and to let his man in the unit know that if he didn't come right back to go to the stash and grab what he had.

"The books sell and you know what we talked about just hold that other thing down and I'll get at you. " Romie was moving fast as ever. He didn't want to miss this work being put into at all. Romie put the books up, then he ran to his man to give him the news and headed for the beef against the D.C dudes.

The entire B-More car had rolled up into Big O and Rob' s unit. They all walked up into the unit where there were around 10-15 other D.C dudes that were just watching T.V., playing chess, and playing cards. They had no idea what the B-more dudes were coming to handle, so since they didn't have a clue as soon as they saw how many B-More dudes there were, they knew that it was major beef with someone. They were never ever thinking that it was in their own car. A few of the D.C dudes ran to get their knives as well, they just wanted to support the B-More car. Romie walked in and everyone dapped him up. "Yo, what cell they in", asked Dre?

"Who ya'll seeing homies, "asked one of the D.C dudes who didn't like the Southside of D.C. niggas anyway. He was from North East D.C...

Dre said, "That nigga Big O and Rob."

"Oh the homies, yea they violated big time," said Romie and the D.C. dudes told them their cell was right there

#1819. The night light was dimmed a li'l bit and Dre walked over and peeped into the cell and saw both Big O and Rob was sitting there high as Fat Charlie. He opened the cell door fast and with the knife wrapped around his hand, he moved just like a pro.

Big 0 was sitting right there at the door on the toilet nodding almost getting ready to tip over. Dre grabbed Big O and began stabbing him in the chest, back, head, arms, and all over his body. Another B-More dude walked over to stab Rob. He tried to get up but the raw dope had taken full control over his entire body and functions. They put the work in on the two D.C dudes who had played with Romie's cellie with the fake books of stamps. As the scene became clear to a few of the other D.C. dudes that were from South East D.C., and who really messed with Big O and Rob, they approached the B- More car to see what was going on. Romie thought that they was trying to run up on them and help their homies out, so Romie just kicked it all off with the rest of the D.C dudes that had walked up trying them like they wanted it. Everyone was slinging Their knives now. It was a lot of bloodshed. One D.C dude ran up and got hit in his eye, while a B-More got stabbed in the neck and the blood squirted way across the unit. The officer had walked back into the unit to catch all of the bad blood in action. The C.O. hit the deuces and the compound was yet again on lock down. Dre had put in that work on Big O and the B-More dude who had Rob had worked him over as well. After it was all said and done there were around 55 people involved in the madness. You had other people that were rolling with the B-More car from other cars involved to. The Shu Lt. had to release a lot of people that was in SHU for minor stuff. They needed to free up some bed space. Everyone was under S.I.S. investigation. Brown Boy knew from the info that Romie has given to him, when he gave him the work and books that were in the stash that something big was going down in a major way. People were stuck on the rec. yard for hours pass re-call due to this bad blood bath. A few others were caught up out of bounds, being in their homie's unit, getting their hair braided and getting haircuts. A few were getting drunk, and some were just out playing poker, spades, and things of that nature. They were all caught up being out of bounds because of this bloody war that Baltimore and D.C. had out because of someone playing games, trying to get over on the wrong car. It's never about the small things or what you have.   Prison is run strictly on respect and once that respect has been violated there's knife play and people are going to war ...

To Be Continued...

Chapter 1
***** Dirty Dirty *****

Everything kicked off in the summer of 1987. Sput was a young nigga just hanging out every day on the block with his homie's from the way. Sput's clique consisted of his li'l homie Smoke Eye's, Man-Man, Sammy, and joy riding Herb. Herb was a very fun cat to hang around, and loved to always drive around in the city in everyone else's cars. Hold onto your seats as I take you on a li'l ride down in the N.O... On Tuesday night Herb had came past Sput's mother's house and asked him if he was trying to make a quick $100 dollars. Sput was broke as ever and Herb had already known that Sput didn't have any money. To top it all off, Herb knew that Sput was still living with his mother and father. Sput's parents didn't want their son hanging out with niggas like Herb, but Sput and Herb had grown up together since they were about 5 years old. Sput stayed sneaking around, hanging out with his main man Herb. That was Sput's nigga right there.

Chapter 2
***** Dirty Dirty *****

Meanwhile, Man-Man and Sammy were taking their thing to a whole nother level. They were both after those girls and trying to make that paper and get their shine on. They made up their minds that they wanted to get that big money. At least they thought they were getting money. Man-Man and Sammy were just selling a lot of weed when they had first started getting a li'l money and trying to get their shine on.

Man-Man said, "Yo Sammy there's no other way for us to come out of the bottomless pit, we have to do us so that we can start buying our own li'l motorbikes and our own cars to drive around in, and then we can start getting any girl that we want, you heard me?"

Sammy replied, "Yea I heard you my nigga, we got a point to prove, that we got it going on and that we are taking really good care of ourselves."

Chapter 3
***** Dirty Dirty *****

Sput figured that he'd just sit back in the cut and watch, take notes, and pay close attention to Man-Man and Sammy, so that he could learn the game and perfect it in his own li'l ways. Then have his game tight too. Man-Man always called him Sput because Sput was only 15 years old, and he stood "6 '1 2", 150lbs. . . . Sput was the skinniest li'l nigga ever, but the boy had the heart of a lion. All of Sput's boyz loved his go-getter mentality. He was always the main one who just chilled and laid back in his style. He was never the one who talked too much, but he observed everything moving in and out, and when it came down to fighting and beating niggas up Sput knew how to throw his hands really good. Plus, he was a pretty boy with the curly hair and as a ladies man, he always, melted the ladies' hearts when he came around them.

Chapter 4
***** Dirty Dirty *****

Sput just knew that he had all the swagger to knock any girl that he wanted to knock, and he always told his boyz that his swagger was like that. There were days when Sput would just sit back in his room and think really hard and he would be feeling bad because he wasn't the average young kid. His mother and father worked extra hard to make sure that their son had everything that he would ever want or need, but Sput just felt that it wasn't right for him to keep on taking from his parent's. One day he went out on his own, because he wanted to go out and hustle and get that work from his main man. Sput went to holla at his man. All he wanted Sput to do was go out on some crazy capers, small stuff like selling a few bags of weed, or going out on capers with Herb to steal cars. Now Sput had to holla at Herb and tell him about this li'l bad dime piece that was drop dead gorgeous. The girl was to pretty, but Sput had wanted to impress this bad li'l honey and take her out to the movies this upcoming weekend.

Chapter 5
***** Dirty Dirty *****

Sput needed Herb's help with the girl, but Herb saw this as a li'l bit of leverage to make Sput go all out on a caper with him. Sput told Herb that if he could help him out, that he would pay him back, but Herb had other plans while he starred at Sput all crazy.

Herb said, "Come on now my nigga you already know that I got your back on this, but at the very same time I really do need you to roll with me tonight and watch my back, plus I'll make sure that you have $200 dollars, and that's for you just to look out for me. Plus, this li'l job that I have to do will pay big, so can I count on you my nigga?" "Oh yea, " Herb continued, " and you can even roll with my car to really shine on the li'l honey you just met. Herb was the smoothest car thief ever. He even had a stolen car so fresh and so clean that one would have never suspected that he was the one behind a lot of the cars getting stolen. Herb had the cleanest car in the hood. Herb was so fast and so good that if you took your eyes off of your car for 15 seconds, it was a goner. Herb was good at what he did.

Herb said, "Sput, I want you to have my back because this caper is big and I really do trust in you. Once we're done you are locked into using my car and getting them sexy thongs off of that li'l honey that you just met. I know that you don't have a clue about a bus, but you are strong enough to stop anyone from getting up on me." Sput just stood there and stared at Herb. He had a crazy feeling in the pit of his stomach, but couldn't put his finger on it yet.

Chapter 6
***** Dirty Dirty *****

Sput knew that Herb talked about the bus because he knew that Sput had them hands. Sput looked at the scene and told Herb, "Oh, this right here is a easy caper right here. Come on then let's get this over with. "Sput knew that Herb would just roll right up into these people's driveway and take their car so fast, but tonight just did not feel right. It looked as though someone was trying to set Herb and Sput up. It appeared that someone had tipped these folks off and gave them the heads up that Herb and Sput were coming. When they got there the lights were on inside of the house. It was very late and these people should have been sound asleep by now. Sput had that gut feeling again and he said, "Yo Herb let's leave this and come back a li'l bit later on."
Herb wasn't trying to hear that crap.

He replied, "No, we are going to get this now, we're already here now."

Sput said, "But it don't feel right, let's come back later on. It don't look good right now."

Herb said, "Yo, Sput what's up with you tonight? Your acting like a li'l wussy." Sput was fuming now and Herb knew what to say to Sput to get him mad at him." Herb knew that whenever he would say things like that to Sput it would make his fist tighten up. Herb saw Sput biting his bottom lip and his blood was boiling. Herb reached under his shirt pulling out a gun and he gave it to Sput and told him to hold it while he put his down for this caper and then Herb said, "Sput, if anyone and I mean anyone comes to that door you better bust a cap into the air as a warning shot."

Sput responded, "Herb, you going crazy."

Herb replied, "Naw I'm going crazy but if you want to be with this new honey that you just now met then you need to do what you got to do and stop acting like a li'l wussy." Sput stood there boiling again, but this time Sput said, "Yo, Herb you got one more time to disrespect me in that name calling fashion and I'm going to whip your butt out here and I mean it Herb." Herb thought for a quick minute and he knew that Sput meant business so he said, "Man, Sput you know that I was just playing around with you, you know that you are not no wussy, but Sput I'm just trying to get this paper and I felt like you wasn't trying to get it with me. I want you to take that pretty li'l girl that you just met out wherever she wants to go to."

Sput stood there and thought for a minute and he said, "You know Herb, I really like this girl so come on let's do this. I'm doing this one li'l caper with you and I'm done.

To Be Continued ...

Chapter 1

***** Why You Hate Me *****

Ring, Ring, Ring, and Shea answered the phone, "Hello."

Tray asked, "What's up baby girl?"

"Nothing much."

"Where you at?"

"I'm at the mall right now getting my clothes for tonight, you know the big fight is tonight."

He said, "I want to see Tyson knock Lewis out."

"Oh yea, I forgot that was tonight. So Tray will I even get to see you at the after party?"

"Yea, I think that I can arrange that for you, or how about I swing by and pick you up?"

"Yea, that sounds like a plan right there."

"Alright then I'll see you later on." And they hung up. Tray felt a li'l weird all day long his so-called main man was acting crazy ever since Tray had came back home getting that paper again. He had been gone for 6 years now and he wasn't faking to make it. He was getting it and Tray had made up his mind that he was going to be the man after doing 6 long years. He wanted to catch up. A year seemed like forever to Tray and it showed heavy. His two brothers were holding him down all through the entire 6 years that he had been down. They were there like true and real family are supposed to be there, holding the man down. They made sure that he had what was needed to endure this bit, and they made sure that his girl, Shea, made it to every visiting day. Shea, was a trooper; she was a "Ride or die" Shorty and she rode the entire 6 years with her man. When Tray came back home it was apparent that his man Sincere had a lot of hate in his blood towards Tray. Tray never ever did anything to Sin. Sin just had it bad from all the bridges that he's burned down. His using and abusing other people; not caring about how he carried others was now taking full affect on him. Since Tray got back home, he was the only one that gave Sin a shot at getting his money back right. Tee-Tee was also buying a lot of weight from Tray. She was rolling, her li'l shop was jamming; pulling in like 2 to 3 thousand dollars a day. Ever since Tray started hitting her with that work she had not looked back at all. Tray was blessing her big time. Sin knew how much Tray liked Tee-Tee and he vowed to come in between what they had going on in the business aspect of things. On the day of the fight Sin was watching Tee-Tee do what she does to get that paper. He watched her making all that money, and when the time came, he ran up into her apartment with crusty Doo-Doo and they robbed her blind. They had their masks on so that she would not know who it was that was robbing her. They tied her up and blindfolded her. Sin wanted to make a point to Tray that he could be touched. Tee-Tee never would have suspected them to rob her. They took all her work and money that they could find. Then Sin walked over to her, untied her, and told her to count backwards from 50 and then she could move. Tee-Tee started counting, asking them not to kill her, and they rolled out. When she got to 50 they were long gone. She ran to the phone and called Tray telling him what had just happened to her and he came to her aid.

Chapter 2

***** Why You Hate Me *****

On cue Sin and Doo-Doo watched Tee-Tee's apartment again and just like clockwork Tray pulled up.

Doo-Doo said, "Let's get him right now."

Sin said, "Naw, not right now my nigga, we'll roll on that nigga later on, I have a plan for him." They rolled out, but Doo-Doo kept on saying that nigga Tray must be messing with Tee-Tee like that. Sin said, "Naw he ain't, not like that, you know that his girl is Shea."

"I thought she was just coping from him," said Doo-Doo.

"At first she was, then they started messing with each other, but his girl is still Shea. Then I thought that it was a stash house for him but that's all her work. I have a plan, "said Sin.

Tray came and gave Tee-Tee some more work and a gun this time to protect herself, and he rolled back out. As Tray left Sin and Doo-Doo pulled up and went to her house as if they had not just left her house from robbing her. Sin knocked on the door, she answered, "Who is it?" Really loud and still mad and upset about what had happened to her earlier.

"It's Sin, Tee."

"Okay Sin, I'm so happy to see you, and she gave him a big ole hug. He walked in Doo-Doo just smiling to himself that Sin had deserved to receive an Oscar Award for this performance.

She looked over and said, "Hey Doo-Doo. Let me tell you guys something real quick. I've had a very bad day today. This morning some niggas just ran up into my spot and robbed me for everything that I worked so hard to get." They both looked at her seriously and said,

"What? You don't know who would do something like this to you? Who do you think that it was?" They said it in a tone that made her comfortable not to think that they would do such a thing like that to her. They made it seem that if they knew or had an idea who it was, they would run to kill this person who had robbed her.

Tee-Tee said, "I don't know who could or would want to hurt me or take my stuff like they did, but I thank Tray because he came right back and gave me a big 8th this time around. He has blessed me this time for real. So I'm all good now." Oh yea, Sin was heated because it seemed like what he and Doo-Doo has just done to her only made her more of a problem than before. Sin lied on Tray and told her that Tray was the one who had put the work in to have her to get robbed. He made her think that Tray was jealous of her and the money that she was raking in.

Sin even said, "So he did it anyway and I told him not to do this right?"

Tee-Tee said, "Do what?"

Sin said, "Tray tried to have me and Doo-Doo to rob you, so that you would be in the rear and be working for him."

Chapter 3

***** Why You Hate Me *****

"We told him no that we wasn't going to be robbing you, and I guess he went on ahead as planned and had it done by someone else."

Tee-Tee was now fuming and she said, "Oh yea, so two can play that game. I'll just set his li'l butt right back up. Watch this one!" Doo-Doo just stood there looking crazy thinking wow. He thought Sin played this part to a "T".

Sin turned to Doo-Doo and said, "Plus we made a vow to never ever hurt you. Ain't that right Doo-Doo? And you know it is what he said back to the question. Well now that you know what has taken place we are going to handle this for you, but Tee-Tee you have to lure him back over here so that we can handle him for you?"

"I got his butt real talk, watch this." She called him on the phone and he answered,

"What it do?"

"It's okay, how about you?"

"I'm good, but I called to let you know that I need more work, it is rolling out here for real. I need you to hit me again I sold all of that real quick."

Tray calmly responded, "I'll swing pass there," and they hung up.

Tee-Tee said, "There it goes then. I bet you he won't make it to see that Mike Tyson vs. Lennox Lewis fight, mark my word on that. I got him on this one." She told them that Tray was on his way back over there. Tray had been chilling all day. He had just left his mark up on Florida Street. He just

54

switched from driving his F-150 truck to driving his '99 Deville. He just got the ole school washed. One of his li'l flings that he had met at the club Premier had called him trying to hook up and spend a li'l time with Tray, she had family in Memphis so she already knew that it was going to be very busy at the Memphis International Airport. Tray couldn't stop thinking about the fight tonight. He had a lot of money betting on this fight. It was getting late now and Tray wanted to hit Tee-Tee again. So right when he was pulling up to serve her and get going so that he wouldn't be late, up walked two gunmen with their shirts covering their faces as masks. Tray still had the car in drive. When they unloaded their guns on him hitting him everywhere. Tray pulled off praying that the Lord would be with him through this trying time of his life. Everything flashed in front of him as he drove, trying to make it to the nearest emergency room. Blood was everywhere, all over the car. The windows were shot out and shattered glass was all in his hair and eyes. He could barely see to get to the hospital that night but the Lord Jesus Christ was with him here. He had someone praying for him. Tray thanked the Lord for saving his life and to be alive and well today. His two brothers had gone as far as putting out a hit on the people that was behind this hit. Word has spread like wild fires about Tray getting hit up. Tray lived to this very day ... More to Come...

Chapter 1

***** Who Shot You *****

"Yo, Black, what's up?"

"Nothing! I'll holla at you a li'l later on," and Black pulled off headed to his block. Dreeka wanted a sub and fries with a good ole half-and-half, meaning that she wanted tea and lemonade mixed together. Black pulled up on Brunt Street. It was a lot of people outside and all the parking spots were filled up, so he drove all the way over to Pressman & Freemount Avenue and parked across the street from Santa Maria's Carry Out.

He then walked over to Penn. and Bloom Street where his cousin Tree was awaiting his arrival.

"Yo, what's up," said Tree?

Black said, "Nothing much, I have to order Dreeka some food real quick."

Black was turning to get ready to go into the Blue Store when one of his other girl's pulled up on the block.

Tiff beeped her horn at Black and he walked over to her car, bent down and kissed her. She had like 7 other girls' that he knew inside the car.

Tree walked up to holla at the girl's that he knew inside of the car. Tree knew everyone in the car. Black turned around and told Tiff that he had to run inside the Blue Store and order some food real quick. As Black walked towards the carry out he started praying because something just didn't feel right with how tonight was going for him.

As Black walked into the store, a dude walked up to Tiff's car to try and holla at the girl's, but none of the girl's we're feeling this dude. He began to curse them out and disrespect them. This dude was angry and out of order. Tree was upset by the way that the dude was disrespecting Black's girl, so he began to take up for the girl's. Tree started beating the dude up pretty bad. A few of the girls had tried to stop Tree from beating the dude too bad, but it was not working.

One of the girl's ran into the store to get Black so he could stop Tree from hurting dude more then he already had. Black came running out of the store after ordering Dreeka's food.

Black ran over to the car where the dude was getting his butt whipped pretty bad. Some of the other girl's were praying for the dude, even while he did what he did to them, they prayed that he would not die right then, from all of the stomping and punching Tree was giving to him.

Finally, Black was able to get Tree off of the dude, and the li'l dude went running down Bloom Street. Black took off a few seconds later right behind the dude. He wanted to make sure that everything was all good with the dude, but Shorty was gone in the wind.

Black turned back, after realizing that he wasn't going to be able to catch the dude. As Black was walking back up to the store to pick up the food that he had ordered for Dreeka, he found himself praying that he could make it through the rest of tonight safe and sound. Black knew that even in his mess he still needed God to make it through.

Tiff was circling the block still trying to see if she could get Black to spend the night with her. Black went into the store to get the order. Black paid for the food, then he turned around and walked up out of the store.

As soon as he took 5 steps, a car pulled up and 3 men exited the vehicle. The dude was back and he had 2 other dudes with him this time. Black just stood there looking at them walk over to him.

One of the dudes that had came back with the li'l dude that Tree had stomped out started yelling, asking the dude, "Who did it, who jumped on you, Yo?"

The dude was looking all around, but Tree was up inside the after-hour joint chilling. The dude pointed out Black and said, "I don't see him, but he was with him." Black was saying to the dudes that he was the one that had broken it up, and he stopped what was happening to Shorty.

The dude kept right on walking towards Black, but he also was reaching inside for something. Black spun around and began to run down Pennsylvania Avenue, heading for Pressman. Black looked back as he was running and he could see the dude covering his eyes and he squeezed the trigger letting his gun rock off; bullets were flying and zipping all past Black's head and body.

As Black was running he could hear the bullets flying past his head. All Black could do while running was pray to God that He would shield him and protect him from dying that night.

As the gun kept on rocking off, one of the bullets ricocheted off of the ground along with another bullet. The 2 bullets hit Black, 1 in the lower leg and the other in his upper hip area. Black kept on running. He felt his side getting kind of warm and he knew that he was hit. He ducked off behind a nearby wall. Then the gun fire stopped, although Black heard another fresh set of shots ringing off, someone else was now shooting.

Someone had come to Black's aid. When Black heard the new gun fire change, he ran to Pressman where he had parked and decided that he was getting somewhere far from all of this madness.

He put his right leg into the car and he sat down. He put the food on the seat as he tried to lift his left leg into the car, but he couldn't. Black physically lifted his leg into the car and rolled out.

Police were combing the area trying to find shooters. Black made it home and he limped into the house where Derek started talking to him right away. As soon as she heard Black enter into the house, she started telling Black how happy she was that he was back with her food. Dreeka could smell her food from the room that Black was standing in. Black put the food and drink on the table. Black had begun to take off his clothes to see if he was shot anywhere up top. Black's entire left leg was turning the color burgundy. Black called into the room to Dreeka and said, "Hey boo, listen I need you to stay calm and don't panic on me."

Dreeka replied, "Black, what are you talking about now, I don't ever be panicking do I?' Dreeka walked into the living room. She saw Black with all of his top clothes off and she looked a li'l puzzled, until she looked down at his leg, and all hell broke loose. She went right into panic mode.

Black said, "I asked you to stay calm for me. "

Dreeka yelled, "What happen to you, Black? Oh my God, all that blood on you, please don't die on me, I need you Black".

Black responded as calmly as possible, "I'm not going to die; look, calm down, and get yourself together. I need you to call my mom and let her know what happened before she hears it the wrong way and comes off the home monitor box." Black's mother was on home confinement. Black wanted Dreeka to call his mom and let her know that he has been shot, but that he was okay! Dreeka called her, but she was going crazy on the phone, crying and screaming. Black got on the phone and spoke with his mom to assure her that he had indeed been hit a few times, but that he would be okay, and for her not to leave the house and get into trouble because she was on a house monitor.

His mom understood his every word to her and she knew that he was indeed okay. Black finished by saying, "Mom, thank you for not going crazy. I'll keep you informed."

"Black, you better call me as soon as you get out of the hospital."

"I will ma," and they hung up.

Dreeka called #911 for help and they arrived in record time. They came in and cut Black's pants off to get to his wounds. When Black had first came home and parked the car, there was not a soul outside, but as soon as the medical people started to roll him to the ambulance the entire street was full of onlookers.

Tree had Tiff and the rest of the girl's drove him to where he thought Black had gone to after the shooting.

Chapter 2

Who Shot You

As soon as Black rolled out to get into the back of the ambulance, girls were screaming and crying because he had gotten shot, and they did not know if he was going to make it or not. Dreeka was at a loss for words; tears were running down her eyes and face; she couldn't stop them from falling. She was also very upset at the fact that so many girls were there to support the man that she loved and cared so deeply for, the man that her life revolved around. The ambulance pulled off headed to University Hospital Emergency Room.

Police detectives swarmed into Black's hospital room asking him major questions about the shooting- - what and who did it to him? As the lady detective walked over to where Black was, she stood out to him. Black tried very hard to remember where he knew this woman from and suddenly it came to him.

Earlier on that day he had been at the car wash getting his car washed, detailed and waxed, and he remembered that she was there at the car wash getting her car washed as well.

She was super fine too Black. He was getting ready to lay down his mack game on her, but stopped as soon as she reached into her pants pockets, and he saw her shiny B-More City Police Badge, and her Glock '9'mm hand gun on her hip. He knew she was the police then. Now she was standing there in his room at the hospital asking him questions; doing an interview about him getting shot.

She asked Black, "Did he know who had shot him?"

Black told her, "I don't know who the shooters were, but I was at the sub shop getting some food, someone was fussing and the shots went off."

She told Black, "Nice try, but we know who shot you already." Black looked at her puzzled, then he asked her, "Well who shot me then?"

She responded, "We're conducting an investigation right now, and I can not disclose that information to you right now. We'll know more details later on. You get some rest, and then she walked away from Black.

Black was just lying there staring into space wondering why in the world would a woman as fine as this police detective want to work a dangerous job like being a police officer.

Black found himself trying to shake her beautiful face out of his mind. Then a li'l pain hit him, and he began to seek God as he so often did. Black began to pray to God. Black prayed for the dude who had shot him. Then he prayed and thanked God for allowing him to see this hour because he remembered the doctor telling him how lucky he was to still be alive. There was another guy right up stairs above him who had been shot in another fight and had the very same gunshot wounds, but the bullets had hit a main artery and they couldn't stop the bleeding.

Black knew from that just how blessed he was. Doctors and nurses were yelling trying to get some order in the hospital. Black had the hospital looking like a night club. Girl's were fighting over who would get to visit him while Dreeka was his wife, and she would first have to leave in order for anyone else to be able to visit with Black.

Black did not have his phone on hand. He wanted to try and stop his people from hunting the li'l dude down ... It might even be a li'l too late.

To Be Continued ....

Chapter 1
***** Urban-Soup/B- More Loyal*****
A Praying Man

"Man, it's pouring down, raining out this joint," said Gena. Trina responded, "It sure is, girl, you know that we have to go slide pass the bar to check up on daddy."

"Yea, you right, I have not seen him in a li'l while now. I know that he misses us. "

Rob and Bill had just pulled up to the new bar that his older son Rico had just brought. Rico was raking in alot of money in the mean streets of Baltimore. Rico was getting it and there were a lot of people trying to hate and take his throne. He had haters that were very salty at him. Rob got out of the car and popped the trunk to get all the bags that they needed to start working on the new bar. Rob had been praying and serving God for as long as he could remember. Rob had just came from church earlier on, before he went to pick up Bill the plumber. Rob had been trying to talk to Bill since they had first had hired him to work in the bar. Rob wasn't going to give up trying to get Bill saved. Rob liked Bill a lot and he knew the talent he had could go a long way, so he vowed to stick with Bill and keep him on the right path. He knew that God gave him a great gift at doing plumbing jobs. They were engrossed in their work trying to get the new bar finished so they could soon have Rico's grand opening to celebrate his success of trying to get up out of the drug game. As Rob was hanging up sheet rock and whistling his favorite song by: J. Moss, "Sweet Jesus," someone was knocking and banging on the front door hard as ever. Bill had the music on and he really could not hear the person knocking at the door. Rob heard it and went to answer the front door. To his surprise it was an unknown man at the door.

He had an umbrella and had on a hood that was covering up his entire face, but it was raining so Rob did not think anything about it or pay it any mind. Rob opened the door and asked the man what could he do for him. The man turned around with a gun in his hand pointed in his face. All he could really do at that time was say a silent prayer, hoping and praying that God would keep him and that the death angel wasn't ready for him just yet.

Rob finally found his voice, and he said, "Please don't shoot me, I'm just here working to fix up the old place, we don't have any money or anything here."

The man said, "Shut up old man," and then asked, "How many of you are in here?"

Rob said, "Me and the Plumber that's all." The man took his eyes of Rob for just one second and Rob knew it was life or death, so Rob moved fast. He was on the man trying to get the gun from him, but was only able to get his finger behind the trigger of the gun so the man couldn't shoot him. They tossed and turned hard, but Rob wouldn't move his finger. Rob started getting tired, and the man was getting tired as well. They wrestled for a good li'l while.

Bill had to take a smoke break, and he thought that he heard a li'l noise, but he kept on smoking. Rob stated calling Bill's name for help.

"Help Bill, help Bill, Bill help me."

Bill heard Rob calling for help and he came running to the rescue. Bill had a li'l pipe in his hands and he ran up behind the man and started hitting him with the pipe. Rob would not let go. Bill kept working the man with the pipe, and finally the man got up off of Rob.

He let go of the gun and he began to run towards the front door that was still wide open from the moment he had came through it.

Chapter 2
A Praying Man

Bill swung the pipe at the man while he was running to the front door and the pipe caught hold of the man's back pack that he was wearing. The back pack dropped to the floor, but the man kept on running, Rob was so mad at himself. He was getting ready to shoot the man in his back, but something told Rob not to shoot and he didn't. Bill came over to Rob and asked him, "Was he okay."

Rob said, "God answered my prayers. I was tussling with that guy for what seemed like hours. He could've killed me, but the good Lord was watching over me."

Rob laid stretched out on the floor thanking God for watching over him and sending Bill to his aid when He did.

Bill called the police, and helped arrived in minutes. While help was on the way Rob and Bill decided to investigate the contents in the back pack. They both were surprised to find that the man had a roll of duct tape, hog ties, blindfolds, and a cell phone. The first thing Rob thought was that the man was on a major mission and that this was not a game. The man had it set up like he was coming to kidnap them. Rob turned in all of the evidence that the man had left behind. Rob then called his son Rico and told him all about what had just taken place at the bar. So Rico told his father that he was on his way. God was protecting Rob all the way through this ordeal.

God is in everything even when we don't feel like He is. He is there! Rob never got the 411 on the phone records, finger prints, or anything else about this almost, kidnapping case.

Rob stayed in prayer even more now that he had, had a chance to witness the power of the true and living God, who will have your back and your front. He prayed that nothing would ever happen like this again.

To Be Continued ....

Chapter 1
***** God Is Never Wrong *****

"A Man That Did Not Believe In The Power Of God, And God's Goodness."

The streets are always made to be run and respected. Everyone has their respect and things are ran according to your power when you're in them streets, but we all must know that God is the Author and King of those streets. They are God's streets! People are out there and in a crazy way they think that them streets are theirs, but the truth is that God's goodness is the best way to run your life.

A man was running the streets one day, but he never gave God His props and he did not trust in God's goodness. He had a crew of goons who did have knowledge of God and knew that they were under the care of the Almighty Creator. The crew one day said, "Boss man, you don't even have to be discouraged about anything, because in everything that God does for us, He makes no mistakes at all. Never ever does God make any kind of mistake."

One day the crew all got together to go to Six Flags Park and on their way there they had a car wreck. My position was to always lay me life down for my boss. I could not prevent my Boss from losing 2 of his fingers in the car wreck, but I did manage to save his life. My actions caused him to still be alive and well, all but the 2 fingers that he lost in the wreck.

My boss was really furious with me and he did not show any kind of gratitude to me for saving his life. I looked at my boss and asked him, "boss, isn't God good?"

My crazy boss said back to me, "If God was really good like you always saying that He is, I would never have lost my 2 fingers in that car wreck."

I replied back to him, "Boss, despite all that has happened to us, I can still stand here and tell you, as I have always told you, that God is still good despite what has happened to us,

He is still always good, and He knows why He has allowed all of this to happen. It is something that we can't see right now, but in due time He will show us what it means. What God always do is perfect, and He is never ever wrong."

My boss was very upset and outraged at me, so he had the other workers to detain me and hold me in a house in the cellar for days. So I was like being arrested by the boss man because I spoke about God's goodness. Later on as the days passed by my boss took some guys out on another road trip. This time some cave men captured my boss man. They were deadly cavemen that practiced human sacrifices. These cavemen had my boss man at their altar getting ready to kill him, but the main caveman came to my boss to check to make sure that my boss had all of his limbs before they sacrificed his body in pieces. The main caveman found that my boss had only 3 fingers on one hand, so the caveman ordered that my boss be released from their cave. They could not sacrifice humans that didn't have all of their limbs. Their sacrifice would be incomplete with him having lost 2 fingers. When my Boss got back from the long days of the trip that they had gone on, he admitted being scared out of his mind and he even found himself calling the God that I had been telling him about.

Chapter 2
God Is Never Wrong

My boss was actually praying to God, wanting to get himself right. He wanted to be saved so that he could know the real true and living God of this world. When my boss got back to the house, he told the other's to go and release me from the cellar where they had been holding me captive. When I walked to where my boss was in the upstairs room, he grabbed me by my arms, cried, and told me what had happened to him. He also told me that he was praying that the God I serve would somehow make a way for him to make it back to me and tell me what he went through. He needed me to help him get the God that I served to hear his prayers and to save him.

My boss said, "God was really good to me today, I was kidnapped and was getting ready to be killed today by some cavemen, but for me missing them 2 fingers from the car accident, the cavemen let me go. But I just have one big question for you Mr.???? If the God that you serve is soooooo good, then why did He allow me to put you in that house in the cellar today????

"Well, boss, I' am ever so grateful that you did lock me away in that cellar, because had you not put me in the cellar today and locked me away, it would have meant that the cavemen would have had to sacrifice me instead of you because I have all of my fingers. So in all things always remember that God is good all the time and that God doesn't make any mistakes at all.

God is so perfect and He is never ever wrong. It is often that we as people seem to be complaining about something in life.

Always about the negative things that happen to us, always forgetting that nothing happens to us randomly, and that everything that happens had its purpose.

So I say this with faithfulness to you reading this: Every morning when you awake, offer your life and day to God, and don't be in a rush. Always ask God to inspire your every thought. Guide your actions, and ease your feelings. We don't ever have to be afraid because God is always right and never wrong. You know why we as people know that this is for all of us? I don't know the answer to that, but God knows it, because He never ever makes mistakes. What we have to do is pray, pray, and keep praying. God is good all the time
.... God Is Never Ever Wrong ..

To Be Continued ....

Chapter 1
Li'l Jonnie

"Come back here right now boy, before I get you."

Li'l Jonnie ran as fast as he could to get out of that house, trying his very best to not have to hear his mother's mouth. He vowed to never ever return home again.

He stopped at the corner, looked back one last time and he said under his breath, "She don't love me anyway."

He walked right along, without a care in the world. His mother, Tammy, tried to do the very best that she could do, but she needed help. She was having it hard as ever right now, trying every day to find a way to pay for her drugs because her mind kept on telling her that she needed it to make it every day. Tammy grew up in the church all of her life. Her mom and grandma stayed on her about the Lord Jesus Christ, but she decided one day that she could do it on her own without God.

She began having sex outside of marriage and conceived li'l Jonnie. Big Jonnie was not saved at all, his only family was the streets and he was a well-known member of the world that runs with the evil ones.

Li'l Jonnie, knowing the history, thought that there was no one else in the family that really loved and cared about him. His best friend, which was his grandma Ms. Sue, had passed away leaving li'l Jonnie to fend for himself. He was lost without his grandma around now. She was all that he had, and she showed him the real true love and heartfelt caring he needed, but when she passed away, he always got whipped, punched, and cursed out. Li'l Jonnie looked for help, but there was no one to turn to. Jonnie went and tried looking for love in all of the wrong places. He resorted to hanging out with a pack of li'l goons that were just like him. All of them were without guidance. No one to love them, support them, talk to them, and show them all of the right ways to do things.

Mark was the shot caller for this li'l pack of goons. Mark had the boyz doing just about everything there was to do under the sun, robbing, stealing, killing, hitting banks, and stealing cars. The devil had Mark doing all of his li'l dirty work through these young boyz who did not have a clue, day in and day out.

Li'l Jonnie was feeling the love and attention that they all showed to him, especially Mark. Mark made things appear to be all love and heartfelt caring and Jonnie felt it was a li'l bit better then what he was used to getting from the mom and dad that he ran away from.

Jonnie felt that Mark cared just a li'l bit more than his parent's did. Mark sent Li'l Jonnie on a mission that would soon cost Jonnie his freedom. Jonnie was hurting and torn down to the point that he would say things like-there is no real God and he went as far as getting tatted up with the numbers 666, just to remind him that he was an outcast, but if you believe that there is a devil, then you must also believe that there is a God too.

Jonnie went on his last caper which caused him to get arrested. He received a 17-year sentence in prison. After doing 3 1/2 years, Jonnie met a man who took a good liking to him.

Chapter 2
Li'l Jonnie

The man showed Jonnie real true love and respect as a man. He told Jonnie about the Lord Jesus Christ and how he used to have a cold heart towards everything and everyone, but when he gave his life to the Lord everything changed for the better.

The man told Jonnie that He was going to have to stay in prison. He would never ever again have a chance at life like Jonnie would. He would never ever again get another chance to walk the streets again. He had two life sentences in prison and he told Jonnie that whatever property he had or left behind, he was going out of this world in a black body bag.

The man was crying and it somehow touched Jonnie. Jonnie was scared now because he knew in his heart of hearts the situation that the man was in could have easily been his.

Jonnie wiped his eyes after the man told him all that he had to tell him. A few years on down the road, Jonnie was saved. He was allowing the Lord to use him in ways that Jonnie would have never ever been able to be used before. The man died in prison and it caused Jonnie to grow closer to the Lord Jesus Christ. The man taught Jonnie that he cannot trust and depend on people in his life or on his own will power. He had to give everything up and depend totally on the Lord to make things fit, Live the life that God has set up for him to live. The man told Jonnie that the will of God is the best will and he had to line up with the Word and allow God to have His way. When doing the will of God, doors and people will open up in ways that only the true and living God can make happen.

Jonnie made parole before his time. As Jonnie rode the bus to his new foundation, he could not believe that he had dodged God, the real, true, and living God, for all of those years. He knew that he had to go through this ordeal in order to meet God this way. The man always told Jonnie that you never ever know your true purpose and strength until you have been through something that only God could bring you out of.

Smelling fresh and so clean, not like the smoke that the devil leaves us smelling like.

God had also blessed Jonnie with a pen pal while he was away doing his time. This woman was a good woman, a gift right from God Himself. It was the daughter of the man who had lead Jonnie to the Lord Jesus Christ. Jonnie was blessed to have a place and new family to go back home to.

Jonnie is now a changed man, living and honoring God, praising the Lord Jesus Christ always. He has gone back and joined the old church that he and his grandma had attended when she was alive and well. He's a new member on the church board, active in saving lives. He shows and gives his testimony being involved in the youth's lives. Both boys and girls, he's mentoring all of the kids that are growing up and living like he use to live. He tells how he use to be feeling, so he knows their pain from what he endured back then. Jonnie can now teach the lessons that the man taught him in prison, giving them the answers to their problems that so many people search for but never really find. The answer is the Lord Jesus Christ! Try Him if you don't believe me. God loves you if you will just open up your hearts and ask Him to come on in. Then you will get a chance to see the true and living God in action in your life and how He, and only He, can make things come together for the better of those that love and serve Him...

To Be Continued ....

Chapter 1
***** Follow Jesus Christ*****

The decision has been made. I'm a disciple of His. I won't look back, let up, slow it down, back away from it, or be still. My past is redeemed, my present makes all the sense to me, and my future is very hopeful.

I'm finished and I'm done with low living sightseeing and walking, small planning, smooth knees, colorless dreams when mines are bright, tame visions, mundane talking, poor giving, and fake goals.

I no longer need preeminence, prosperity, position, promotions, or popularity. I don't have to be right all the time, first all the time, at the top all the time, praised, or rewarded. I now live by His presence alone, learn by faith, walk by patience, lift up all my prayers and I labor by God's powerful hands. My face is set. My gait is fast; my goal is to get into Heaven. My road had always been narrow. My way is rough. My companions are few. My God is reliable. I'm focused and my mission is very clear.

I cannot be brought, compromised, returned, lured away, turned back, deluded, or delayed. I will not flinch in the face of sacrifice, hesitate in the presence of adversity, negotiate at the table of the enemy, ponder at the pool of popularity, or be caught up in one's maze.

I won't give up, shut up, or let up until I have stayed up, stored up, prayed up, paid up, and preached up for the cause and movement of my Lord Jesus Christ.

I must go on until He comes. I must be giving until I drop, preaching until I can't glorify Him no more, and I must be working until He stops me, and when Jesus comes for His own, guess what He won't have no problem recognizing me.

......"If any man come to me, and hate not his father, and

mother, and wife, and brethren, and sister, yea, and his own
life also, he cannot be my disciple"
     Luke 14:26

Chapter 1
***** You Jump I Jump*****

I could say that I love you more than enough times to fill a million rivers deep with water, but why let the free words love fall silently into the silent whispers of the wind, when your hearts ears are imprisoned by thoughts of mistrust?

Like cheap whiskey, mistrust rots every center and every vital aspect of love and life. Suffered we have not from a lack of love. The question of love has never ever spilled blood in our bed.

My mistrust of you is the only bridge which led to our separation of love and trust. I loved you from the deepest corridor of thoughts and dreams. You filled my life with rushing waters from the broken dam of all hopes and dreams that one could ever manage to imagine.

Am I scared? Yes! Am I afraid to jump? Yes! All of my life I have dreamed of that love like the Titanic movie, that "If you jump, I jump" type of love. The type when a real man will race his thundering horse across the fields of battle for the sole sake of the one woman worth dying for.

Prison has never been about 4 cement walls and a steel door. Prison, for me, has been a place of redemption from the wickedness of my own soul! The streets would have certainly killed me, because life re-creates physically that which you live for mentally. I mistrusted my own self which caused life to place me in the predicament of mistrusting other people in my surroundings.

Prison has been about trust to me; trust of my own ideas, dreams and abilities; trust in God and Jesus Christ my Lord. Jail has been about, if not you, then who? If not now, then when? Who would have changed my life had I not accepted Jesus Christ?

78

When would I have made the decision if not today, and if not right here, right now? No way possible could I change yesterday, or make you and me forget the pains of yesterday.

Trust is always meant to be challenged and love is meant to be fought for. Trust me with a test; make me fight for you, and I'll strangle the wind of it's own breath!

By: Christopher White Jr.

Chapter 1
Why You Rape Me

"Shoot, girl, my dag on feet are killing me. Did you like the service this morning better then all the other ones we have went to?"

"Ma, I love all the services that the Preacher have.

It really keeps me away from the house and all the hurt and pain that I be going through, Ma."

"Well, what are you going through, you know that you can talk to me."

"Ma, I have told you about it and you just keep on looking at me like I be lying to you."

"Oh, that's what you on again. "

"Yea, Ma, because you know he be hurting me but you turn your head."

"I'm not having this conversation with you again."

Melvin was sitting, watching, and waiting for Cindy to yell out what she always yelled every day before she would leave for work. "Tee, I know that you mad at me, but the good Lord will make a way. Tee, make sure that you cook dinner for us, I'll be back. "

Tonya said, "Mommy, do you have to leave me, you know what I told you and I'm scared to death, Mommy, don't leave me pleaseeeeeeee's Mommy".

Cindy said, "Girl, don't talk like that."

Meanwhile, Melvin was listening to their entire conversation. Tonya went upstairs to pray. She knew that it was her only defense for what was ahead of her. She prayed

"Lord Jesus, please save me and don't allow this man to keep on hurting me, in Jesus Christ name . . ..Amen."

Tonya came back down stairs to talk Cindy one last time before she was to leave for work. Tonya said, "I'm telling you Mommy, Daddy keeps on touching me and I'm really scared." Cindy said, "Girl, shut up, before I beat your butt. "

Cindy walked into the living room, bent down and she kissed Melvin and said, "Baby, don't worry about her, you know that she on them med's again. Don't pay her any attention."

Melvin looked at Cindy's eyes and it seemed like this would be the very last time to ever see this kind of love. Cindy looked ever so seductive to Melvin at this time, but his mind was running and thinking about what he wanted to do to Tonya.

Cindy asked, "Melvin, what are you going to do today?"

Melvin said, "I don't know yet, maybe I'll watch the football games with the guys, I don't know yet."

Cindy said, "Well, I have to run to work, I'm late

Church ran longer today and Tee got me all worked up too. I'm late as ever."

She kissed Melvin and she ran out to the car.

Melvin ran to the window quickly as he so often did, not realizing that Cindy was up to something today. Today was Sunday and she was off from work, but Melvin was thinking with his penis head, instead of his mind's head. As usual the old curtain moved back fast as always. Cindy saw it like she always did, but this time she had a plan of her own.

Chapter 2
Why You Rape Me

Cindy was fed up and tired of her 15-year-old daughter accusing her boyfriend, Tonya's father, of raping and touching her, taking advantage of her.

Tonya was counting backwards from 100, and just like clock-work, she heard Melvin's footsteps coming towards the bathroom where she had run to hide earlier when Cindy was not listening to her cries. Tonya was in the bathroom hiding, praying that God would somehow intervene from Heaven on her behalf.

Melvin walked up yelling for Tonya, saying, "Come on out now, sugar bun, where are you?"

Tonya yelled at him, "Daddy it's not right, you're hurting me.

Melvin said, "Shut up and open up this dag on door before I kill you and your mom tonight."

Tonya yelled out the door, "No daddy, leave me alone, no don't kill my mommy, and Tonya opened the bathroom door.

She always made it to the number 26 on her backwards count before Melvin got to where she was hiding at. It was always the number 26.

Tonya knew that once she got to 26 he would be right there at the door.

Cindy had driven off, leaving for work, at least that's what Melvin thought she did. But Cindy drove off and she did a double back this time around. She snuck into the house from the back door and was able to hear and record everything that Melvin said to Tonya loud and clear. Cindy was so hurt hearing this coming from the man she loved and admired for all these years. She could not stop crying, but she was on a mission to free her li'l girl from the rape that was getting ready to happen to her.

Melvin said, "I love you, Tee."

Tonya said, "Daddy if you love me you would not be hurting me like you be doing."

Tonya continued, "Come on, Daddy, and get this over with before mother come back. I hate you, Daddy, and you are going to pay for this one day. You know that God is watching you right now. Lord help me pleasseeeee's."

Melvin slapped her because he did not believe in God and he hated to hear her calling on a God that never showed up for him when he was going through all the hurtful situations that his father had put him through. He told her to take her clothes off and to get naked. Tonya started crying, Melvin was yelling at her. Out of nowhere in walked Cindy with her 9mm hand gun pointed right at Melvin's head. Her face was soaking wet from all the many tears that she had dripping from her eyes.

Cindy said in a low voice, "How could you, all this time Melvin, really, how could you take away my baby's innocence like this?"

Melvin just stared at her dumb founded and looked at the gun in her hands. Then he looked at her with a smirk on his face and said, "Girl, put that dag on gun down and get your butt on over here and join us before I kill you with my bare hands. "Cindy started to cry even harder now, she pulled out her cell phone and dialed #911. The emergency operator answered ...."911 emergency, how may I place your call, Police, fire department, or ambulance?"

Cindy said, "I have an intruder in my home and he has raped my li'l girl, my address is" and as she was trying to give the operator the address for help, Melvin started to get loud with her, screaming and trying to grab for her. The 911 operator said, "Ma'am are you okay?"

"Is the intruder still in the house?" Cindy replied, "Yes."

The 911 operator started screaming into the phone that help was on the way. She kept on asking Cindy, "Ma'am are you there, Ma'am, Ma'am, and the operator was getting scared for Cindy's safety now. She said silent prayers that help would arrive in time and that she would not lose the caller. The operator heard Tonya screaming, "Mommy, Mommy, no Mommy" .... and then all you heard was boom, boom, boom, boom, and then everything was all quiet.

To Be Continued ....

Chapter 1
I'll Die So That You Can Live

Ring, Ring, Ring. "Hello", said Chris. "Yo, what time is it," asked Chris?

Bo said, "It is 7:05 a.m.."

"Man let me go", What? I have to go and wake Dream up. She late for school. They hung up quickly.

Chris got up really fast, he showered, and he started calling for Dream to get up.

Dream screamed to him, "I'm up already Daddy."

Chris said, "Dream, you are late for school baby, and we have to move fast. You know that school is very, very important, right?"

Dream screamed back, "I know Daddy, I know." Dream asked Chris, "Daddy do you really love me?"

Chris stood there for a minute trying to figure her out. He answered her, "Why of course I love my li'l angel very, very much.

Dream said, "Daddy, I read in the Bible where Jesus Christ died for the world. Daddy, am I the world to you?"

Chris was really starting to get a li'l nervous now because Dream was getting deep with him today. She had never been this tough with him and talking this much about serious things such as (Love) and (God). Chris answered her back, "Yes, Dream, you are the world to me. Dream, my li'l angel, can I ask you where you are going with all of this?"

"Nowhere Daddy, I just thought that I would ask you because I always be hearing a lot of people using the 4 letter word (I LOVE YOU). Daddy the 4 letter word everyone be abusing is very, very serious."

They both showered, ate quickly, and ran out of the door to Chris's car.

Today just felt so weird to Chris, he could not put his finger on what was ahead of him, but in due time he would know why he was feeling the way he felt.

Dream's cell phone rang 3 times, and she answered it. "Hello, her girlfriend Tay was joking with her about the li'l get together that they had planned for this upcoming weekend. Dream had a secret that only she and Chris shared.

The world would never ever know what that was unless Dream told them about it. Dream was so ashamed about it because she had to take all of this crazy medicine.

Chris was driving like a bat out of hell, moving too fast and way over the speed limit.

Tay told Dream that li'l Mickey was in love with her. Dream said, "What? I'm only 15, and what does he know about love Tay?"

"Huh Dream, you can't ask me that, you have to ask him that." "I will; just wait until this weekend."

The next thing you know a UPS truck came from out of nowhere and crashed head-on into Chris's car. Tay started yelling into the phone, "Dream what's that noise that I hear?" Then Tay heard Dream screaming. She could also hear Chris moaning like he was in a lot of pain as well. Tay kept on screaming into the phone, "Dream, what happened, what's that noise?" The crash was really bad. The emergency call was made.

Police and emergency help had arrived along with the emergency helicopter. Chris was going in and out of consciousness. He began to hear a still small voice saying to him, "Do you love me, would you die for me?"

Chris immediately started saying his prayers, and as he prayed, John 3:16 and 17 kept coming to Chris's mind.

16. For God so love the world, that He gave His Only Begotten Son, that whosoever believeth in Him should not perish, but have everlasting life. For God sent not His son into the world to condemn the world, but that the threw Him might be saved. Chris was thinking very hard about God.

A doctor walked over to Chris. He asked, Mr. White can you hear me?"

Chris said, "Yes. "

"Do you know where you are right now?" Chris replied, "No."

The doctor said, "You and your li'l girl were in a bad accident earlier today, and she is lying lifeless right now. Do you understand what I have said to you?"

Chapter 2
I'll Die So That You Can Live

Chris said, "Yes, I understand you."

The doctor said, "She needs a heart. I have something else that I would like to discuss with you. It is very, very important in this life or death situation. Are you ready Mr. White?"

Chris answered him, "Yes." "Do you love your girl?" "Yes, I love her to death."

"Would you rather live and let her die, because we found out that she has HIV, we found her med's."

Chris was all the way awake now, looking as serious as ever now. He thought for a quick second, then it all hit him like a ton of bricks. The questions and all the talks he and Dream had been having. Now he knew why she kept on asking him them questions and why he was feeling so strange. The feelings he had been having were really strange and he knew what it all meant now.

Chris now knew what true love and real sacrifice really meant to him. He laid there and wondered why Dream asked him so many times whether he loved her, and how she went into depth about just how serious that 4 letter word really meant. Chris now understood why John 3:16 came to his mind like it did.

Chris looked at the doctor and said, "Doc you can't save us both, I do understand."

"No sir, we can't save both of you. Only one of you can live with one heart. It would be impossible to make it happen."

"Well Doc, I just need you to do me one big favor and tell my li'l girl that I really, really, loved her and I hope that my faith can show her my love. I want to sign the papers to give my life for my li'l girl's. Take my life, doc, give her my heart, I'll live the rest of my life through her."

To Be Continued ....

Chapter 1
***** Immediate Release *****

"They have been calling you boy, you better get on home. There it goes again. What is it, you hear them calling you. Stop playing, "Said Jeff, to Black again.

"Inmate James got to his counselor's office, they told him, "Mr. Brown you have been released on parole, get your things packed up, come and get a phone call and you are a free man." I laid down on my bunk for a few more minutes to get this right in my mind. I thought of the Flower Lady the entire time. How I wanted to make love to her so bad. I called her and told her I was on my way back home to her and she went crazy. I told her that I would there in a few hours, she was at a loss for words and said to me, "Okay I'll be waiting your arrival."

She was calling me Memphis.

"Okay Memphis, "she replied back to me.

It was snowing pretty bad outside, the weather was crazy outside. I thought that since it was snowing that bad the airlines would have been closed by now, but to my surprise they were still flying planes out. As the plane flew it was moving pretty fast, but not as fast as the beats of my heart, thinking about this woman that I love and cared so deeply for. The flight attendant seemed to notice my anxiety, even as my wife-to-be was back at home trying to get the mood set up for my arrival and what was ahead of us as a whole. She was all too anxious. As I thought long and hard about my wife to be, I could almost inhale her intoxicating scent of Halo Boy that she always smelled so good wearing! I just wanted to feel her silky caramel skin, and look into her sexy big brown eyes. After my call to her, I was sure that she was already awaiting my arrival all day long. I had even sat there and tried to imagine what she was doing while I flew on the plane.

She was back at home carefully in preparation. She had rose petals all over the place, all over our room, the bed and the floor, and the scented candles were burning all over the room, which gave the room a nice li'l glow. All the candles had the room illuminated, and the scent smelled so very good. This was our li'l love zone. The candles had a flickering light that gave the room an atmosphere of pure serenity. She had our favorite song playing in the back ground, "I'm Ready" by Alicia Key's. While I flew on the plane, in my mind's eye, I could see my love bug waiting silently in our jacuzzi, trying really hard to contain her impatience as she started to flip through page after page of a magazine. She was feeling giddy inside as each minute was slowly passing by. She kept on imagining that she heard me knocking at the door.

Then I finally came to her. I saw her coming to the door through the window. She opened the door and just stood there staring at me. I was smiling, and we stood face to face, not touching, the space between us like an island of warmth. She began to unzip my jacket and she hung it up. She was so nervous that she poured herself a glass of fine wine to relax her mind a li'1 bit. I never took my eyes off of her beautiful face. I reached out and cupped her sexy face and we just gazed deeply into one another's eyes, just savoring our togetherness. I tilted my head down to hers and pressed my burning lips to her sexy full lips with that pretty shiny lip balm she wore all the time. We held the kiss for dear life and I wrapped my powerful arms around her sexy, shapely body and pulled her against my chest and her nipples were so hard. Boy were those jugs hard. By that time a familiar heat had risen up through my entire body. She pulled away from my embrace and without saying anything she led me by the hand into the bedroom. She sat me down on the bed and bent over to remove my shoes. When she told me to stand up, I did, and she pulled the rest of my stuff off of me and laid it all on top of that special chair that she kept in the room. When she would fall asleep, one of the kids would always place her lap top on the chair since she was so weary being up all those many nights typing her poor li'l heart out on the Corrlinks email. She started kissing my chest. She was enjoying the sweet anticipation of my love. She breathed in the comforting scent of my sex and she smiled. Oh, how she wanted to jump my bones and wrap her mouth around the head of my wood. I could tell just how badly she longed to caress my balls and feel the li'l trimmed hairs tickle her face. She had a lot of discipline though. She stood up and led me to the steaming jacuzzi that she was in before I had even arrived at the house.

When she saw me sitting down comfortably she took a bar of dove soap and washed me up. I stood there with my wood hard as a brick and even in her face. She kept on washing away the jail scent that was stained in my skin for all of the many years of being away in that place. She rinsed me off, then grabbed under my balls, and she increased the pressure and started stroking my wood, feeling it get harder and harder and bigger. I moaned a low whimper as she rubbed the top of my wood with her fingers.

I felt some heat hit the top of my wood, and it was already in her mouth. It was so big and thick but she liked the new challenge of taking it all in her mouth the way that she was doing it. She went up and down a few times. I could not hold the penned up pressure any longer and I released my big load that I had been holding in for all those years of being away from her.   She swallowed every last drip-drop.   She sucked a li'l while longer until every drip drop was in her mouth, not leaving any of it to go to waste. I placed my hands on her beautiful cheeks and pulled her towards me and held on to her for dear life. I loved this woman!

She then got into the tub with me and I held her, just savoring the feel of her silky flesh against mine, me just looking into those big brown eyes. I got hard again a started moving my hips against hers. Her breathing started to quicken, as I lifted her up and carried her to our bed. She had nothing on, and her skin was flawless. I wanted her so badly, but I wanted this to last us forever and a day. I wanted to make her love me more than when we used to email, more than when she came to see me in person on them visits, I wanted this to be forever and to please her like she had never ever been pleased in her entire lifetime. Her big eyes were beckoning me already and I kept on kissing her and smelling her hair. I loved to kiss her lips, and lick her lips to make our kissing that more impassioned.

I kissed her eyes and nose, her ears and neck, and she sighed deeply when I kissed her neck that was her hot spot all of the spots. Her titties were nice and big, but they were firm for me only. I did tiny li'l circles with my tongue on one nipple and rubbed the other nipple with my hands. She gasped for air when I slightly pinched one nipple and bit the other one with gentleness. I knew she was super wet and I could not wait to taste her sweet juices. I kissed my way down to her tummy. I smelled how good she smelled as I licked my way to her super wet coochie. I was kissing the insides of her shapely thighs. She gasped again as I stuck my tongue inside of her wetness and hit the deepest passion ever known to her. I drank her cum greedily as my tongue went deeper and deeper inside of her. Her back arched and her hips rose so that her coochie could meet my mouth. I then blew a li'l bit of air on her clit and she went crazy, out of her mind. The candles had her wetness looking so good. I could not wait no longer. She spread her legs wide open for me as I put a pillow under her butt just so that I could improve my entry angel. The head of my wood found its mark and I slid inside of her a li'l ways, then I pulled it right back out of her. I slid it right back in slightly, a li'l further this time, but not all the way in yet. She was trying to hold my wood inside of her with her coochie muscles, just begging me and telling me that she needed me in her. I held off on eternity longer and then I gave it to her all the way her breath left her momentarily as she shivered with intense feelings of pure and great pleasure. I worked her coochie, moving slowly in and out of her. She was squeezing and loosening her vaginal muscles around my wood causing feelings to take place that I had never ever experienced.

As we made love, I kissed her full lips, then her nipples and from her titties, back to her mouth. Her eyes were a blissful, glassy, pleasurable looking scene. She told me that she did not know if she could last any longer, and that's when it all hit me. She was screaming, "I'm cumming baby, I'm cumming baby, please don't stop, it feels so good, it feels like I'm going to burst wide open. I'm cumming again.

I kept right on beating that coochie up. Faster and faster I went. I pushed her over the edge as I gave my last deep stroke, then we came together this time around. We both did

not know whose orgasm came first to cause the other's to come, but we both felt a river that was running from where we were joined together as one. We laid there and stared at each other for dear life. I was still deep inside of her. Slowly, and very gently her heat rose yet again. She rolled over and got on top of me.

She said, "How?"

I said, "How what?"

"How did you get so hard again, so quickly?"

She just started to ride this horse wildly, crying loudly, that she was cumming yet again. I looked at her sexy caramel face as she started to cum calling my name over and over again, all sense was gone. She was deeply in love and did not have a clue as to what she saying right then. She was encouraging me to cum with her again. After she came again she laid down on my chest and as I slowly pulled out of her coochie, I heard a small moan slip from her mouth, a li'l bit of disappointment escaping her mouth. She wanted to keep it going all night long, but I was drained, just fresh out of the Fed's. I just laid there cradling her face, wrapping my arms around her, making it warm with our body's heat. We were intertwined and we slept and dreamed of more intense love making to come....

To Be Continued ....

***** B-More Loyal/30 Years Before Dishonor*****

Captivating with non-stop action, Christopher White Jr., in his Inaugural debut, vividly walks us through the mean streets of the Number #1 heroin infested city of Baltimore City Maryland. You really got's 2 B-More Careful, because yeah there's most definitely a lot of money to made in these treacherous streets, but here's a place were very few niggas can survive.

The infamous "Black" somehow makes these mean streets of B- More his backyard and "Black" strategically climbs his way all the way up 2 the very top, ducking the haters, handling his foes, driving all the finest cars, getting all of the women, and bringing unity into a drug world where it's nothing but jealousy, envy, and a rack of cut throat niggas, each man for himself and God for us all.

Is "Tony" really "Black's" right hand man, look at how a man rise and fall. "Apple Sider" gives lessons, but he gets off track, do he get back? "Black's" girlfriend "Dia" is all of that and some, until the test of time comes her way. "Penny" is the brains behind everything. "Chuck's" envy is caused by someone, but who? Money is power and every clique is on a mission to get to the very top. Your life for your friends. The Feds are all over the Reservoir Hill community. Who gets indicted, is there a rat in the pack. That's why it's just so dag on hard 2 find those that will "B-more Loyal" .....

Chapter 1
*****B-More Loyal*****

In the beginning it was my mother, my two sisters, and I. Everything kicked off in 1989. When I growing up it was all bad.

One day my man, "Apple Sider", said, "Black I'm tired of seeing you looking and dressing like that. You know that I got that work for right, plus it's 60/40. "

My mother had always told me to stay the heck away from the drug game, so I always said in response, I'm good "Yo."

I was just lying, knowing good and dag on well that I really needed a big break in my life. My shoes had big ole holes in them, running over, leaning to the side, so my shoes were what we all would call "being on the half." My sister's were on the half right along with me. Everyone was always on us so hard, cracking their li'l funny jokes.

This was going on in school and just about any and everywhere else we went. Through his blood line Black always had that killer hustler inside of him. Every day after school he went down to the Stop, Shop, and Save Super Market to bag and carry different people's bags for all kinds of small change. Sometimes depending on how far Black had to go before he would reach the person's car or house would earn dollars. Black started growing real tired of just carrying bags and making small change, so one day he went and had a sit down with his mother "Penny", about the street life and selling drugs. "Penny" knew about everything there was to know about those mean streets of Baltimore.

She ran the streets every day and every night. Penny explained to Black everything that there was to know about the street life. She schooled him on the rules to being a street hustler. The most important #1 rule and code of the streets was that Black had to become a man and always stand, as well as be able to hold his own. The code of the streets is always, if you ever get locked up out there hustling, selling drugs, or whatever it is that you think you want to do in those streets, you can't tell on anybody. Be a man go do your time and get back home.

Penny asked Black, "So are you really ready for what's out there in that street life?"

Black looked into his mother's eyes, with tears in his, that he would not allow to fall and said, "From the looks of things, Ma, I better be ready for this so called street life, because the truth be told I'm tired of starving some nights and not having new shoes and clothes, and everybody cracking their li'l jokes on us. I see now, Ma, that I have to go out and make it happen for myself, because it sure don't seem like it's going to just fall out of the sky for me. So yea, Ma, I'm really ready for the so-called street life."

That night Black made up his mind that it was now or never. Black and his two sisters, Lisa and Chrissy, had all slept in the same bedroom for many years. During the night, something was very different, because Black was crying to himself and both of his sisters could not seem to understand why their big brother was crying. Chrissy and Lisa both got up out of their bunk beds and came running to their brother's side to comfort him, but to their surprise Black was crying tears, no doubt about it, but they were tears of pure joy. Black knew what was ahead of him and his soon to be future. He knew that once morning came it would be the end of all of his struggling days.

Black sat down and told his two sisters all about his run in with the dude Apple Sider, and also his talk with their mother. How she put him on point and her schooling him to the street life. He also told them how he was just so tired of not having and seeing them doing so badly. Black knew what his next move was going to be and he had his mind set on hitting the block bright and early in the morning. Black did not know anything about the street life or the drug game, but he was very strong, very eager to learn, and come up out of the bottomless pit.

Every morning Penny would be yelling at the top of her lungs for the three children to get their butts up. They need to wash up, brush their teeth, eat, and get ready to go to school. As she entered their room, to Penny's surprise, Black was nowhere to be found in the house.

Penny asked her daughters, "Where is ya'lls brother at?" They both looked at each other and said, "Ma, we have not seen him. He was here with us last night, right before we all went to sleep."

Penny said, "That dag on boy is really going to make me hurt him."

Once everyone had gone to sleep, Black had gotten up, leaving the house earlier then usually, so that he could catch up with his dude, Apple Sider, right before he opened his shop. Black came walking down the street calling out to Apple Sider, "Yo Apple, what's up?"

Apple heard someone calling him, he saw it was Black. Apple answered, "Oh what's up Black, you sure out here mighty early in the morning aren't you? What's the deal?"

Black looked into Apple Sider's eyes and said, "Yo, I'm ready to get this money."

Apple Sider looked at Black, then said, "Yo, I knew that you had that killer hustler's mentality in you. Black you know something?"

"What?"

Apple Sider said, "I have been waiting for your arrival for a few months now."

From that day forth Black never ever looked back. Black started getting money, slinging that coke 60/40, left and right. Black was going hard in the paint, hand to hand, getting his shine on hard. While hustling Black's only line that he would quote to people was, "Yo, I got them big blues right here;" meaning that he had them tall glass vials of coke, fish scale to the very top. Big blues was what all of the junkies, meaning the people who used the drug that Black was handling with the blue tops on them. Black had that good, good. One day while on the block Apple Sider told Black that before he knew it those 60/40 packs would have him sitting fat in a minute, just make really sure that he put some money up for a rainy day.

Apple told Black that rainy days would come, and that he just had to be prepared for them when they did come his way. Black heard it all, but didn't take heed or listen to Apple. Apple Sider was trying to teach him about rainy days. Black didn't listen to him. Black was killing the game. He started shopping, buying new shoes and clothes, keeping himself well groomed. plus, taking care of his family. Black even went as far as buying himself a car. It was '88 Nissan Maxima that he had copped from down in V.A. Everyone went down V.A. to buy cars.

As long as you had money you could get anything, any kind of car that you wanted. All you needed was the cash. Whose ever name that you wanted the car's title to be in, it was done. Black was shining, getting plenty of girls and starting to just spend his money all crazy. He started slacking on the block, getting to relaxed, comfortable, chilling, and partying. One day he went to his money stash and he only had $250 dollars left to his name. He had a lot of brand new clothes, shoes, girls, and a car. Black was never taught how to manage his money correctly and right now he was learning a valuable lesson.

Black sat down and thought really hard for just a quick minute, and it all hit him like a ton of bricks. It all started to make perfect sense to him because he finally knew now what Apple Sider was trying to tell him and teach him about when he told him about them rainy days. From that day forth, Black made up his mind that he was going to buckle back down again and get this money back right again. What Black really didn't know was that when it rains it pours down like crazy. He went to see Apple Sider so that he could get back on again with the 60/40 packs, but Apple Sider was now off too, meaning that he was chilling at the time that Black really needed to get some more packs from him. Black was furious, not knowing who else or where else he could get some work from. So Black had to just go on home that day. He kept on wondering where he had gone wrong. He kept on counting that same $250 dollars over and over again, but then an idea popped into Black's mind as he thought of his other dude who was getting money real heavy on the streets of B-More. His name was T-Mac. T-Mac was the man for real. He had all kinds of cars, jewelry, and girls; he was known for doing it really big. So Black Saw T-Mac driving by the very next day and he flagged him down and explained his situation. He told T-Mac what was up and what he was trying to do, but the problem that Black had was that T-Mac didn't deal in small nickel and dimes, or small weight. Black climbed up inside of T-Mac's Bronco truck and they drove around for a li'l while. Black explained himself, while T-Mac contemplated if he was going to allow Black to get some money with him or not. T- Mac finally told Black that he would help him get back on his feet again and get some money again, but that he had to keep on copping his work from him only. Black shook T-Mac's hand to seal their deal.

T-Mac told Black to give him $200 dollars and he would sell him a quarter ounce of coke. Black reached into his pocket and gave T-Mac the $200 dollars, which now left him with $50 dollars to his name. Then he had to go to the vial store and buy two packs of vials which cost him $30 dollars. Black now had just $20 dollars left. Black was thinking out loud and said to his self, "If only I would have listened to

Apple Sider about these rainy days, I would not be at this point right now. But I can't cry now because setbacks like this come with the game, at least that's what Black kept on telling himself.

Black went on home that night and his mother, Penny, was very happy for her son and his two sisters were even happier that their big brother was doing his thing, at least that's how a lot of things appeared to everyone who was just looking in from the outside. Black only had $20 dollars left from the $250 dollars. They both needed $10 dollars for their school lunches for the week and just from Black's outer appearance he couldn't say no to his two sisters. As the weeks passed by Black grew smarter and smarter. He started stacking his money fast and hard this time around. Black would take baths and showers, change his under wear and socks, but he would always put the same clothes right back on.

One day while he was in grind mode, Black met this girl named Dia. Dia was so pretty, sexy, and bad. Everyone in the hood wanted to holla at Dia, but it was just something about Black's swagger that just made Dia melt inside. Black always loved to listen to slow music and he would always carry his small tape recorder with him. His favorite song was by the group. Color Me Bad "I Want To Sex You Up". Little did Black know, but that was Dia's favorite song as well. Dia use to always chase after Black trying to take his recorder from him, so that she could hear her song that he was rocking to. Black and Dia had started to grow to be mad cool as the weeks passed by. Black was now back, focused, still in grind mode, still getting that money, but stacking it all this time around.

Dia liked Black so much that one day she surprised him. She walked up to him and planted the softest and sweetest kiss ever on Black's lips. After that kiss, Black was in love with Dia. They exchanged numbers and used to stay up at all hours of the night, just talking on the phone and listening to each other just breathe. Black and Dia had grown to be inseparable. One-day Black asked Dia to make their relationship official, for her to be his girlfriend. He needed her love and loyalty more than anything else in the world. Black had other li'l friends that he met, but it was never anything serious like he was about Dia. She told Black that she would be the one for him and that she would love him and stay true and loyal to him. Word was spreading around that Black was involved with a new girl name Dia. Dia was way more than a dime piece and all of the other girls had started to wonder what was up with Black, if Dia was so in love with him. Black went from that one quarter ounce, to a half, from a half to a whole ounce, then he went to 2 ounces, from 2 to 4 1/2 ounces, to 9 ounces, to 18 ounces, and then Black just took off from then on. Black didn't look back; he didn't realize that he was now copping 2 kilos of coke from T-Mac. He honored his word to him and Black kept on copping from T-Mac. Black was all the way back on his feet now.

Black got his own apartment. Black took care of everyone that he loved, his girl Dia, his mother, and his sisters was all that he had. Black had started switching cars and he was all the way back on top of the world again, but this time around he was to be for real about his paper. Black was now officially a boss. Everything that Black did was all coming from him getting money from where he grew up at on Whitelock Street and Lakeview Avenue. Black knew other dudes that he had grew up with, who also was getting a lot of money, but Black was set apart from all of the rest. He was getting his own money. Black did not have any partners or crews; he was a one man's army.

Chuck was a go-getter as well. He had a lot of goons on his pay roll and his team was taking down big, but nobody could ever count Black's money. Black was never pressed or concerned about what everyone else had or was taking in. Black didn't have time to be worrying about anything or everyone else, but his own shop and how big his team was raking it in every day. Sampson was another dude that was getting a lot of money from up on Whitelock Street. He was getting money from back in the early 80's, so it was hard to try and count his money as well. Sampson was a millionaire easy, nobody up on Whitelock Street had ever been on his level.

Tony was a nerd. He's what you would call a school boy because he didn't have a hustling bone in his body. He didn't know anything at all about the street life, but Sampson went on ahead and took Tony in and he'd forgotten all about his school work. He just came straight off of the steps getting money with Sampson.

Ricky, Yummy, Ty-Ty, Terrell. and Calvin were all running with Chuck and they were all getting a lot of paper. They all had nice big cars and were doing their thing. Every last one of Chuck's goons were eating really good, and they all had nice, bad girls. Black had girls was an understatement. Black had too many girls, but he always tried to do his very best to respect Dia who was his main girl. Sampson had a nice fleet of girls as well, but Sampson's problem was that he always seemed to fall in love with every girl that he met. Everyone was from this Reservoir Hill area. As the years kept passing on by, Black somehow ended up befriending Tony and they hooked up together and they branched off to a whole nother area. Black was well known all over. Black and Tony started running a shop in another part of Baltimore City.

One-day Black had gone to holla at his man that's from up New York City, and his name was Big Steady. Now Big Steady is taking down like $100,000 dollars a day easy. He was big boy for real, and his crew of goons were on a set time frame. Big Steady only came out every 3 months, only on check days. Since Black knew Big Steady's hustle schedule he wanted to know if he could slide in his hole until his shop was up and running on its own. Black and Tony had now officially

moved up to the big leagues, no more coke, because it was too
slow. They were copping bricks of Boy, meaning heroin. Black
was sometimes called D.J. because he was known for mixing
and cutting dope so well that people were passing out on it,
which made more people run to get it even more. Big Steady
told Black that they could use his hole to get their shop up and
running well.

Black and Tony stayed busy giving out tester's almost
every day. All you could hear is Black's workers yelling the
name of their dope out.

"Dot out, Dot out."

That's what the title of the dope was called and people
who were spending their money asked for the best dope by the
name of the dope that people got. The very first day that they
came and opened shop, they made $7,000 dollars which was
cool for the very first day, but word was traveling fast about this
new dope called "Dot."

Word on the streets was that Dot was the bomb. The
money was steadily rising with each and every day, and in a
week of being out and in Big Steady's hole, Black and Tony
were making anywhere from $40,000 to $50,000 dollars a day.
One day when Black came out he had decided that it was now
time to move out of his man's hole and move to his own block.
Black posted up with one of his workers and they started re-
directing all of the drug traffic up to his new block which was
on Pennsylvania Avenue and Bloom Street.

Upon moving his people, he went and thanked his man
Big Steady for looking out for him. Black tossed him a bag of
nothing but $100 dollar bills for using his hole. Black grew up
not having real friends, especially since dudes always hated
Black's swagger for no reason at all. Black was known and
well respected all over the city of B-More, from East to West,
South to North. Black and Tony has left from up on Whitelock
Street. They had the entire Reservoir Hill area under

investigation. There was a lot going on up on Whitelock Street, but Black and Tony didn't have a clue as to what was going on up there. They kept on hearing about all kinds of beef and different shootings that was happening up on Whitelock Street, but they were focused on where they were jamming at, making $50,000 to $60,000 dollars a day. They had no care in the world about what was going on up on Whitelock Street. Black was now climbing back to the top of his game extremely fast. Everyone in the city was trying to holla at Black. He was becoming the king of the hood.

Chapter 2
B-More Loyal

Dia was so in love with Black. He always whined and dine her to the fullest extent. Every now and then Black would stay in the house and make slow, sweet, passionate love to Dia. Dia had one of the baddest bodies that God had ever created. It was a body that other girls envied; she had a body to die for. Whenever Black and Dia went out anywhere, like to the malls, to the movies, to eat, on trips, or anywhere out of town, Dia's presence always turned heads. Guys and women took double takes at Dia's beauty. She was 5'6", 140lbs, a solid brick house, with long black hair that came down to her butt. She had light brown eyes, perfect white teeth, bow legged with a gap so wide that you could see behind her for blocks. Dia was very beautiful, sexy, pretty, and a true diva and queen in her own little ways. Dia was so pretty that other girls don't even exist around her and she's the woman that Black had created for himself. Black and Dia would make passionate love for many hours and nights on end. Black loved Dia more than anything else in the world.

One day Dia beeped Black and put in her special code #01 followed by a few #911's, which let Black know to hurry up and call her right back. It was an emergency call. When Black called Dia right back she answered the phone crying but Black didn't know that Dia was crying tears of joy. Black heard his baby Dia's cries and he went into a fit of rage, his heart beating extra fast, now. He tried to remain calm cool and relaxed, but he just couldn't contain himself. He spoke real soft and smooth to Dia through the phone.

Black asked her, "Dee Dee what's wrong, why are you crying, did someone hurt you?" Please talk to me Boo Boo. Dia was sniffling and she remained silent for like a minute and then she spoke to Black and said, "I missed my period, and I'm scared and really I don't know what to do from this moment on."

On the other end of the phone, Black was relieved and so happy taking in each word that Dia had just said to him. He knew that Dia's and his lives from this point on would always be joined together forever. Dia missing her period meant only one thing, and that was that Black was getting ready to become the father of his first child. Black was so overjoyed and happy with the good news that he's just received from Dia that he called up his partner Tony and shared the great news with him. Tony was very happy for Black.

Tony was Black's right hand man. Tony was 6'1", 159 lbs. He's a pretty boy, light skin, light brown eyes, tall and skinny, but Tony is cut up like a bag of dope. He was a very handsome dude and he turned a few girls heads every now and then, but Black was the real dude behind all of the women.

Black was 5'11", 175lbs., dark skin, very handsome, and sexy. He had 5 golds in his mouth that he kept blinging at all times. He had a nice body and he was maintaining his physical build really good. He had one of the meanest mack games when it came to knocking other's dude's girls by accident and he even knocks girls for dudes as well. Black is a nice piece of work in all areas.

Black's life was just moving so fast that it was really hard for him to define the real love from the fake love. He didn't even know who was who out in them streets. In due time, however, everything and everyone must reveal itself. That's the law of nature.

Ecclesiastes 3: God said there's a time for everything. As the weeks kept passing by Dia's belly kept on growing and she was indeed pregnant by Black. She was at the market one day and she ran into Black's sister, Chrissy, who was very happy to see Dia.

Chrissy would always say the same thing to Dia every time they saw each other.

"Girl, I haven't seen you in a month of Sunday's, where have you been at? Oh, I know now, you need to keep them legs closed and stay out of that dag on bed, you and my brother. Look at you all big and stuff, carrying my li'l niece or nephew. I'm so happy for ya'll."

Now Chrissy wasn't bad looking either but whenever anyone came into Dia's presence or space bells always went off. Chrissy was 5'10", 155lbs., nice breast and brown skin. She was cute, favoring Black a lot, but she was a girl. She had a phat booty, big legs, and she wore a size 3 1/2 or 4 shoes. Dia and Chrissy did their food shopping together. As they were going from one isle to the next, Dia asked Chrissy how was Penny doing because she hadn't seen her in li'l while. Chrissy told Dia that Penny was cooling and wondering how Black was doing.

Chapter 3
B-More Loyal

Penny hadn't seen her son that much here lately, maybe in traffic every now and then. Penny was really starting to miss her son Black. It seemed like the only time that she ever got to see Black was when he was either bringing her some money or ripping and running the mean, hardcore streets of Baltimore City.

Penny still had a few things jumping out in the streets too. She was still the master mind and the one who blessed her son, Black. She gave him the green light and the game so that he could go out and become the man and hustler that he was right now. Black was always very, very thankful for his mother Penny. She taught him everything that he needed to know to make it.

Black's father's name was Big Clifford, aka Big Cliff, but Black had always hated his father with a passion. Black's father is 6'2, 190lbs., brown skin with 3 golds in his mouth, 2 up top and 1 down at the bottom. It's kind of strange that Black has 5 up top and 1 at the very bottom just like his no good father. Big Cliff never spent any real time with his children, nor has he ever brought his children anything, but a serious void in their lives and in their hearts.

Big Cliff was the reason why Black had to start hitting the streets of B- More so hard, getting all of that dope money, because he had to grow up and become a man at such a very young age, with no father figure. Black vowed to never abandon any of his children once they were born. His father, Big Cliff, left a broken family shattered into so many pieces that could never ever be repaired or put back together again. Big Cliff was nothing in Black's eyes. It was really bad blood between Black and his father. Black just really couldn't understand how a man could just up and leave his children the way that his so called father did his 2 sisters and him. Black was really hurt that his father did that, he made Black grow up without a father figure. The sad part was, Black's father was able to be a dad to them. Black's father wasn't in prison or anything, but it was amazing at how strong Penny had been for her children. She was an extra /supermom as Black called her. Penny was mom and dad all in one person. Cliff didn't have alibi as to why he wasn't a father to his 3 children by Penny. He left Penny to struggle on welfare and whatever money she made on those streets of B-More.

Right after Chrissy and Dia parted ways to go to their respective houses, Chrissy was pulling up and parking her car which she had brought. She had a new Honda accord. Chrissy had just parked her car when her drunken sister, Lisa, was pulling up right behind her, driving like a bat out of hell. Lisa was 5'8 -200lbs., with brown eyes. She was cute since she looked like Black as well. Lisa was kind of on the chubby side, big titties, and super phat butt. Her titties were a size, 44DD, and she could most definitely knock a dude out with those big jugs, but Lisa loves that bottle to death. All she wanted to do was drink 24/7 a day. She drank for no reason, and she always stirs up a whole lot of trouble all of the time. Black never liked to give Lisa any kind of money, because all she would do with it is spend it all on her beer. If Lisa wasn't drinking she was cool as a fan. Black hated seeing his sister Lisa in a drunken state. She would get drunk and cuss any and every one out. Lisa didn't care who you were she would cuss you out so bad, and be ready to fight.

After Chrissy got all of their bags out of the trunk of her car, she went in the house and put the food away, then she called Dia up to make sure that she made it back home safely. Dia's phone rang like 6 times before she heard big brother's voice cut in saying, "What it do?"

Chrissy was so happy to hear Black's voice that she just repeated what he said to her, "What it do then?"

Black instantly busted out laughing at her for trying to always imitate the way that he talked. All of the women that Black cared about loved how smooth Black was when he did anything, even when he talked to them.

Chrissy spoke first, "What's up Big Bro?"

Black just smiled and said, "You know me, just out here getting this paper and trying to keep it coming."

She said, "That's what's up, anyway did Dia make it back from the market safely?"

Black told Chrissy that Dia made it back safely and that she was in the kitchen putting the food away. Chrissy told Black about seeing Dia's pregnant stomach, carrying her li'l niece or nephew. She asked Black, "How come you didn't hip me that you had a li'l shorty on the way?"

When Chrissy asked Black that question concerning his li'l Shorty on the way, it brought back a flood gate of old memories about their no good, lying half a man father, Big Cliff. Black's mind had drifted off back to when he was li'l shorty, and they all were living on Lexington Street. The house had an upstairs and down stairs bathroom, living room, dining room, and kitchen, plus a nice size basement.

One day when Black was a li'l shorty he came down the back steps of the house so that he could use the down stairs bathroom to take a poop, and low and behold, Black found his father sitting on the toilet with a needle in his arm. Black was in a state of shock because this was not the hospital that they were in. They were in Black's house in the bathroom. Seeing this for the very first time in his life he was scared to death, and Black just took off running, and he never even looked back.

To Be Continued ....

About The Author

My name is Christopher White. I 'am 37 years old, and I'am from Baltimore, Maryland. When I grew up in a single parent home, my mother was battling with substance abuse. This led me to rely on the streets for guidance, not having any positive role models, had caused the start of my adult life to lead me to prison. I thank God for loving me and allowing me this time to get my life right. God has used this setback as a major come back so that He could get the glory through my Urban/Christian Novel's that I have penned.

God has birthed in me a gift to write great books to help our world to see that people can change. These books show my negative actions that have positive results. As a ex-drug dealer, I know it was the Holy Spirit that changed me. My books present a message of how God was working in my life while I was still in my mess. My goal right now is to bring about a spiritual awareness and to build a great spiritual kingdom for those who have experienced the same journey such as I.

Yours In Christ

114

Quick Order Form

Make Money Orders Payable To:

You can follow me on Facebook@B-MoreLoyal to keep up with the books that are on the way to a store near you, "B-More Loyal.30 Years Before Dishonor"

Email:Urbansoup2020@yahoo.com

Please send the following book(s):

___ B-More Loyal 30 Years Before Dishonor $12.99

Shipping To:

Name:_____

Address:_____

City:_____State:_____Zip:_____